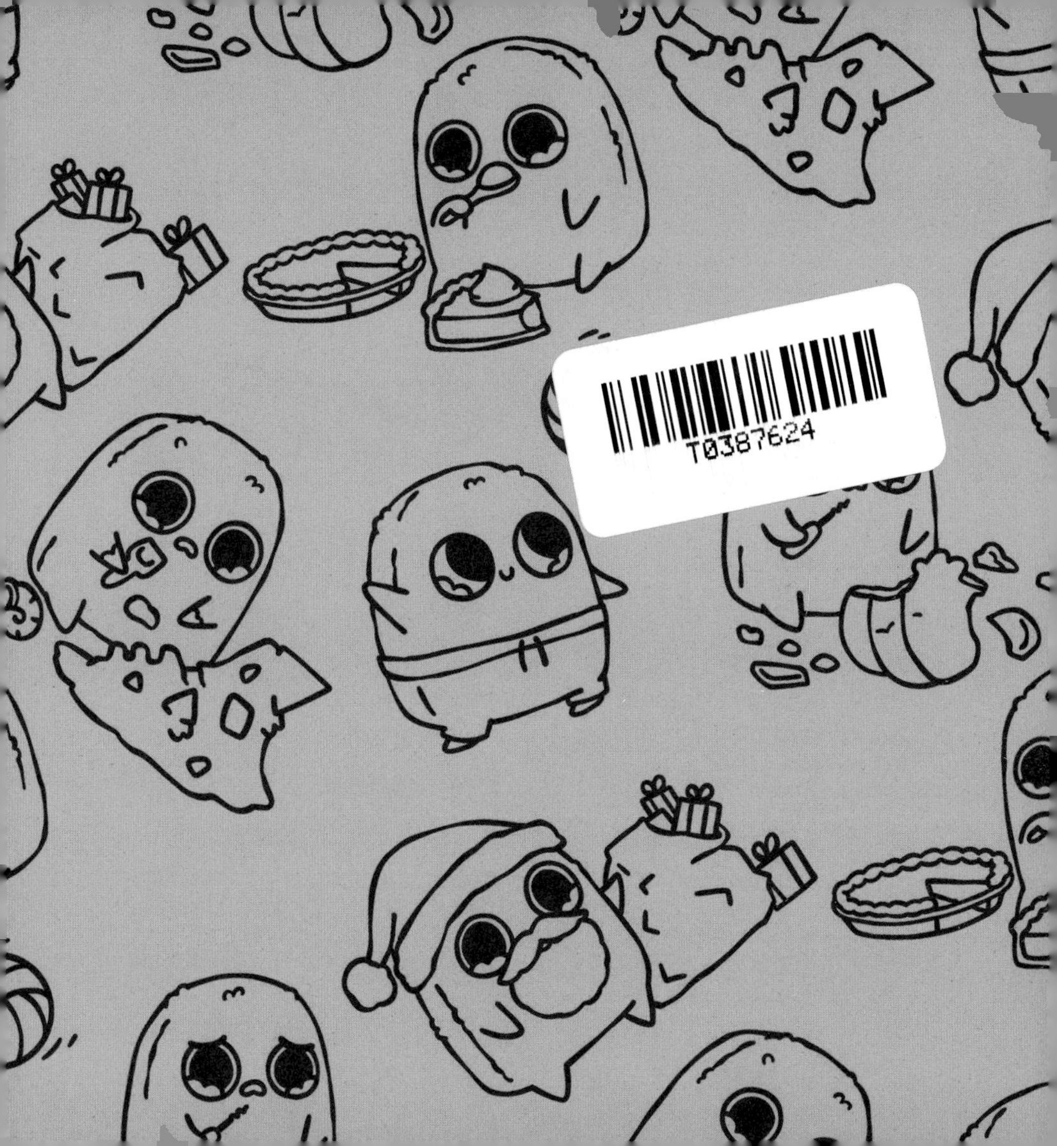

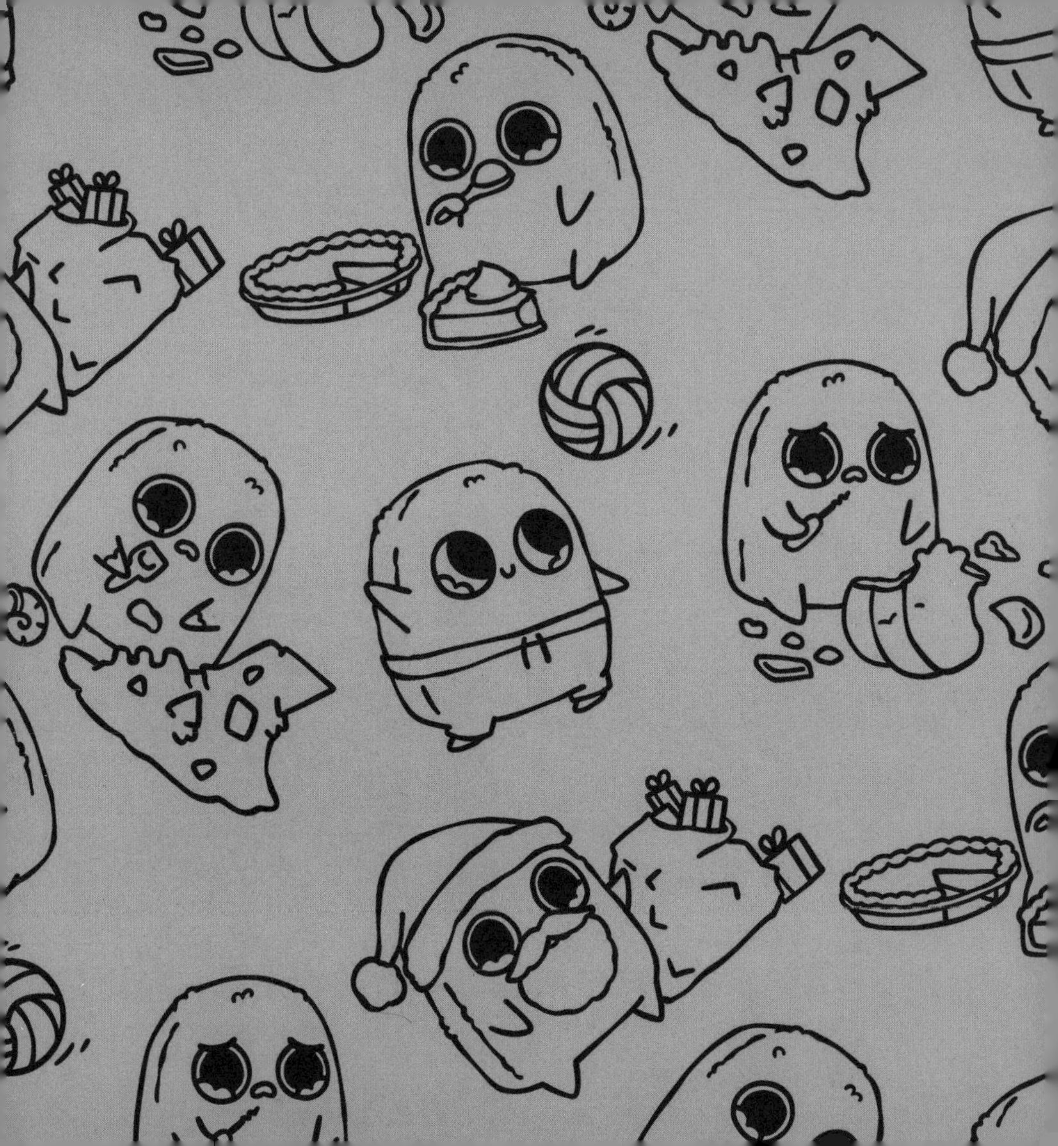

SAD NUGGIE

SAD NUGGIE
LIFE IS
SWEET AND SOUR

By Sad Nuggie

Illustrated by Anastasia Sevastyanova

Andrews McMeel
PUBLISHING®

Sad Nuggie: Life Is Sweet and Sour copyright © 2025 by Sad Nuggie Ltd. All rights reserved. Printed in China. No part of this book may be used or reproduced in any manner whatsoever without written permission except in the case of reprints in the context of reviews.

Andrews McMeel Publishing
a division of Andrews McMeel Universal
1130 Walnut Street, Kansas City, Missouri 64106

www.andrewsmcmeel.com

25 26 27 28 29 TEN 10 9 8 7 6 5 4 3 2 1

ISBN: 979-8-8816-0027-3

Library of Congress Control Number: 2024947928

Editor: Hannah Kimber
Art Director: Julie Barnes
Production Editor: Kayla Overbey
Production Manager: Chadd Keim

MIX
Paper | Supporting
responsible forestry
FSC® C016973

Andrews McMeel Publishing is committed to the responsible use of natural resources and is dedicated to understanding, measuring, and reducing the impact of our products on the natural world. By choosing this product, you are supporting responsible management of the world's forests. The FSC® label means that the materials used for this product come from well-managed FSC®-certified forests, recycled materials, and other controlled sources.

ATTENTION: SCHOOLS AND BUSINESSES
Andrews McMeel books are available at quantity discounts with bulk purchase for educational, business, or sales promotional use. For information, please e-mail the Andrews McMeel Publishing Special Sales Department: sales@andrewsmcmeel.com

Dedicated to those who keep on going even when things feel impossible. You got this.

Contents

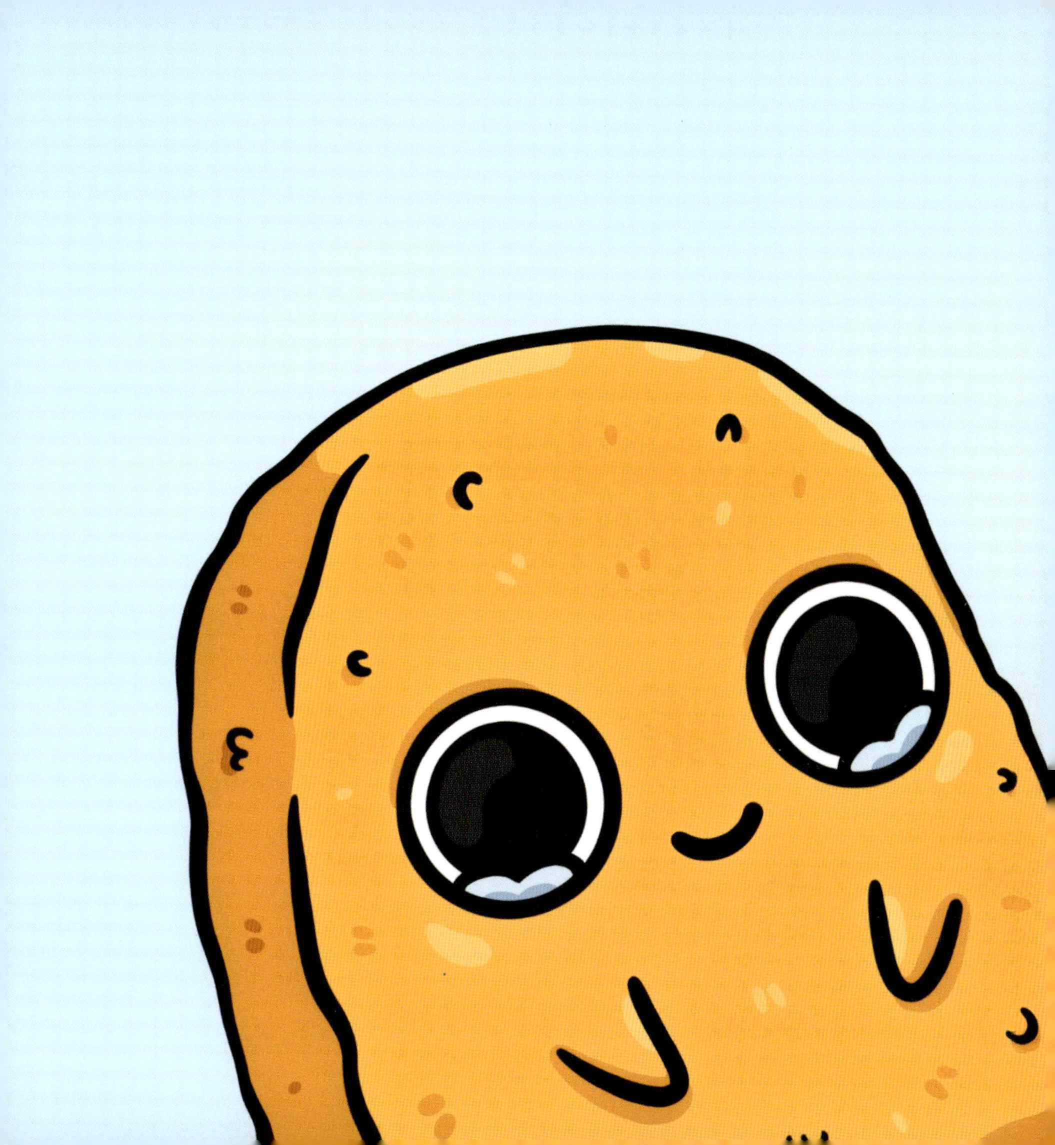

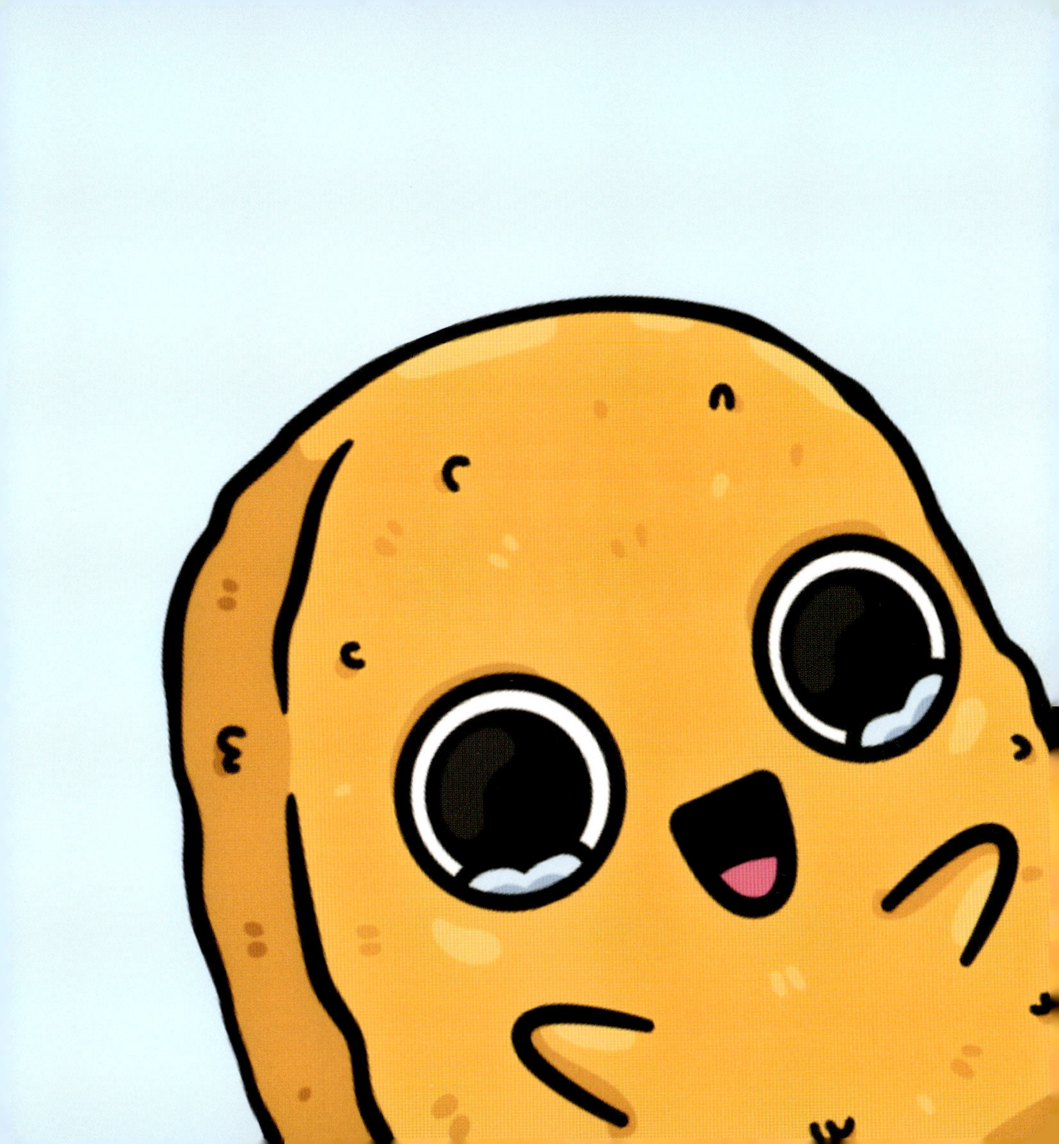

CHAPTER 1

NEW CITY, NEW NUGGET

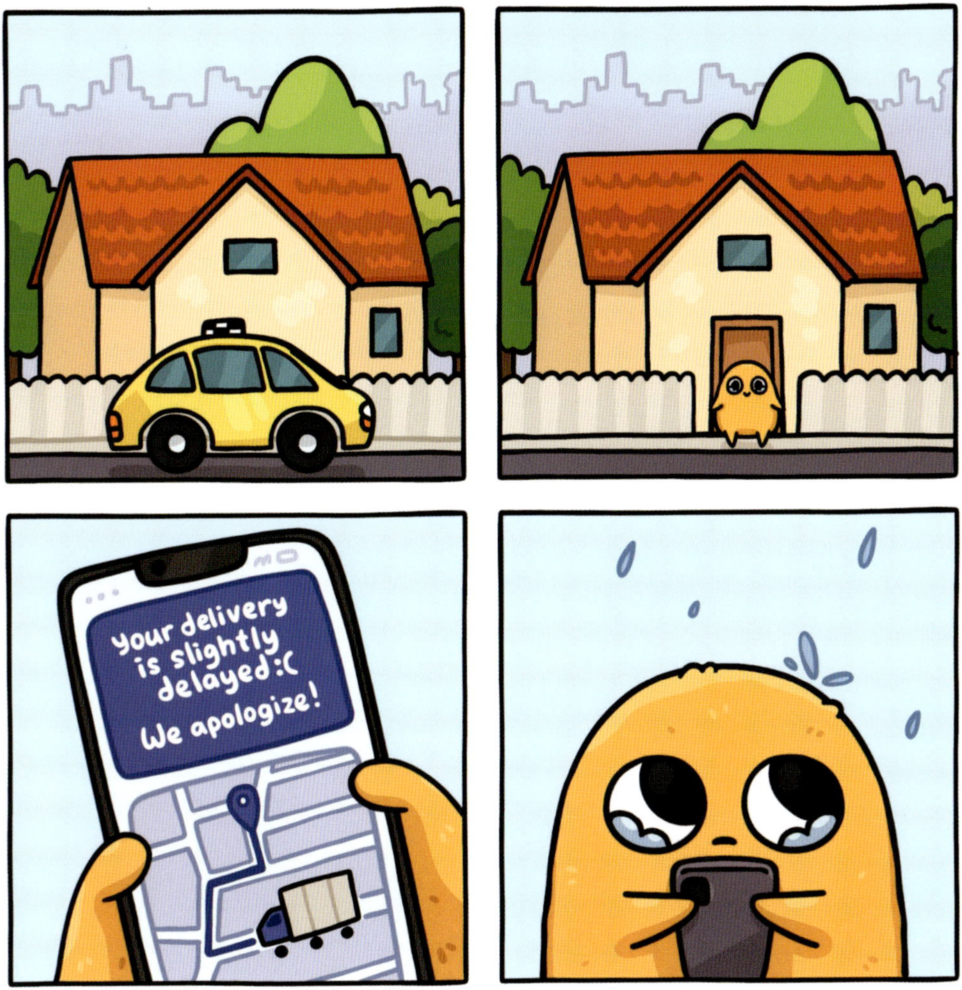
your delivery is slightly delayed :(
We apologize!

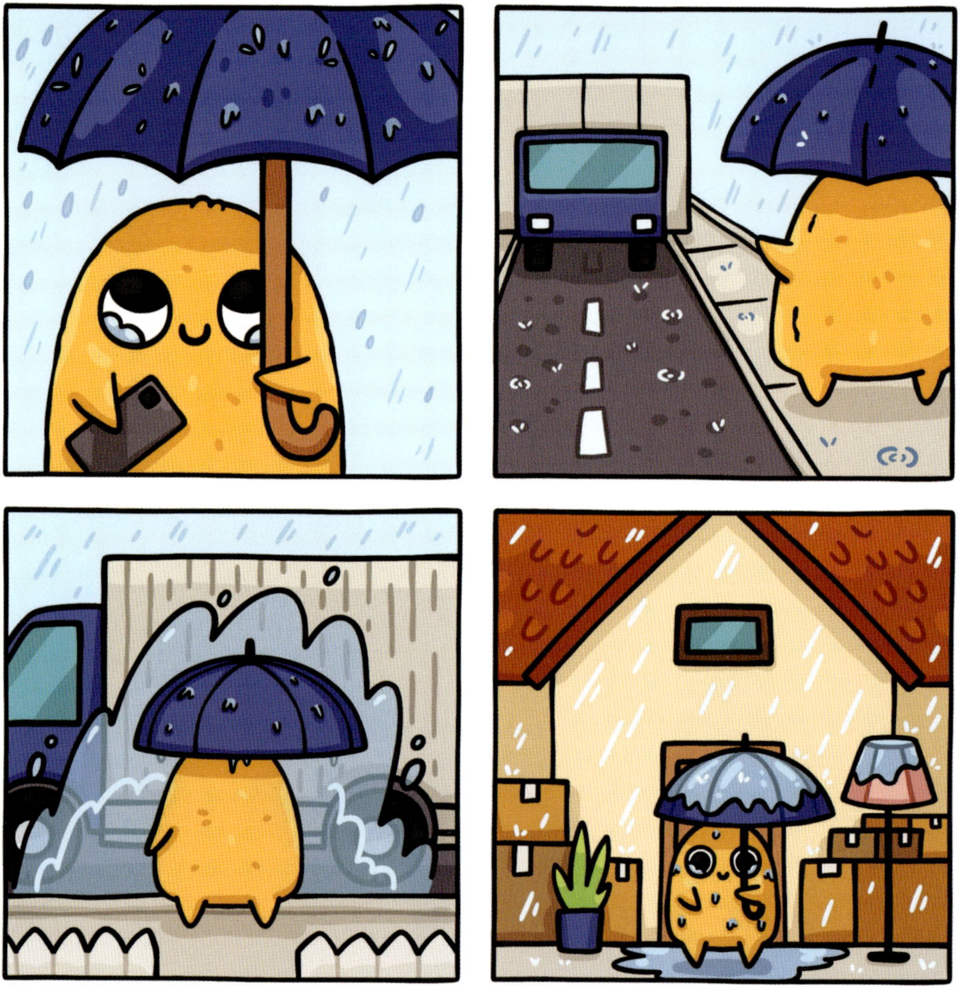

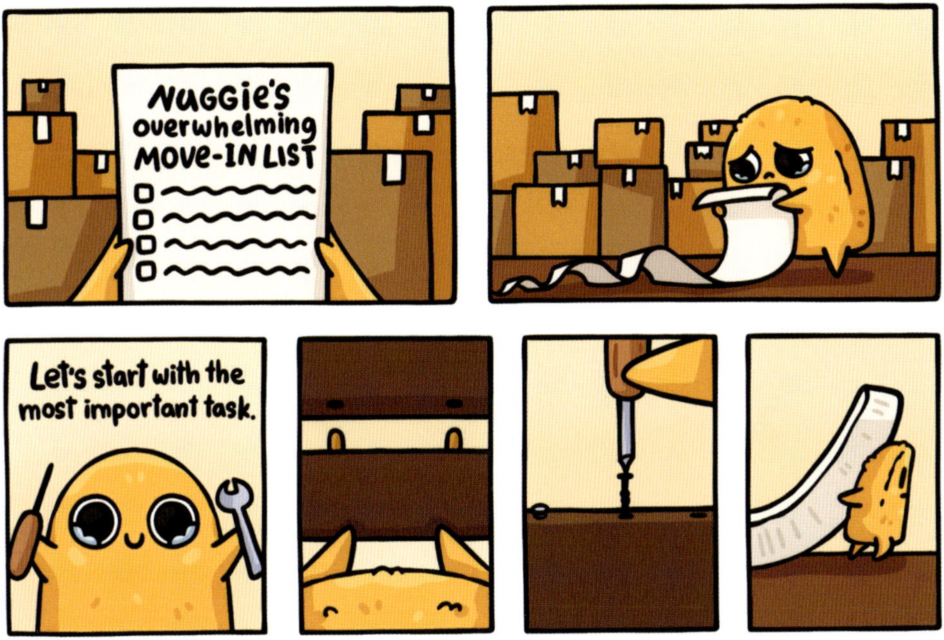

NUGGIE'S
overwhelming
MOVE-IN LIST
Let's start with the most important task.

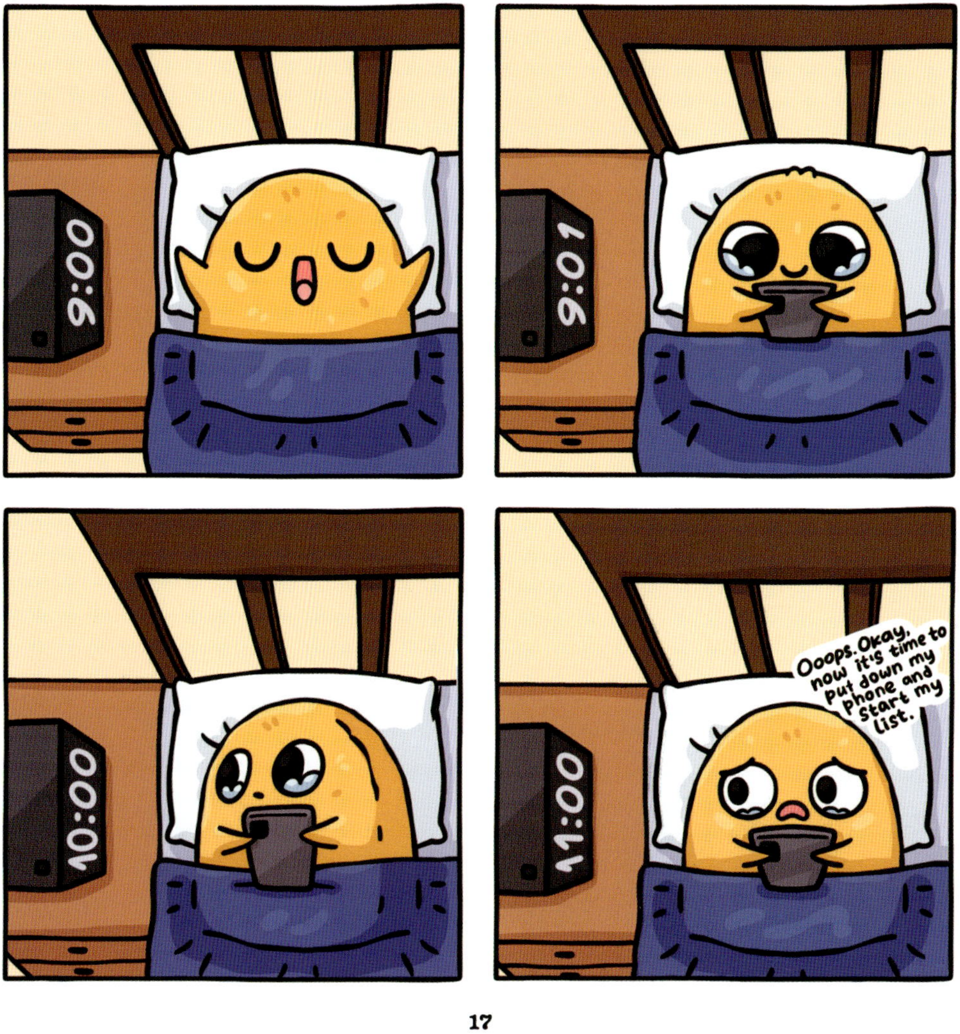
Ooops. Okay, now it's time to put down my phone and start my list.

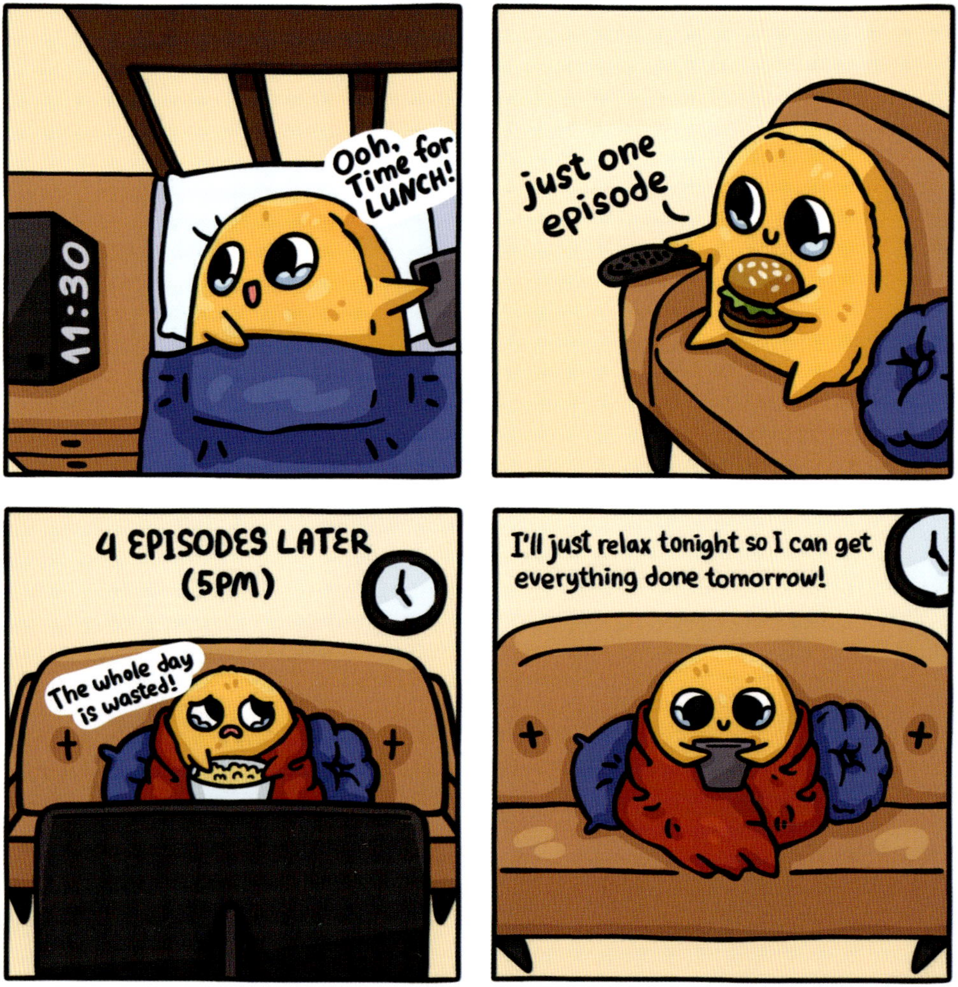
11:30
Ooh, Time for LUNCH!
just one episode
4 EPISODES LATER (5PM)
The whole day is wasted!
I'll just relax tonight so I can get everything done tomorrow!

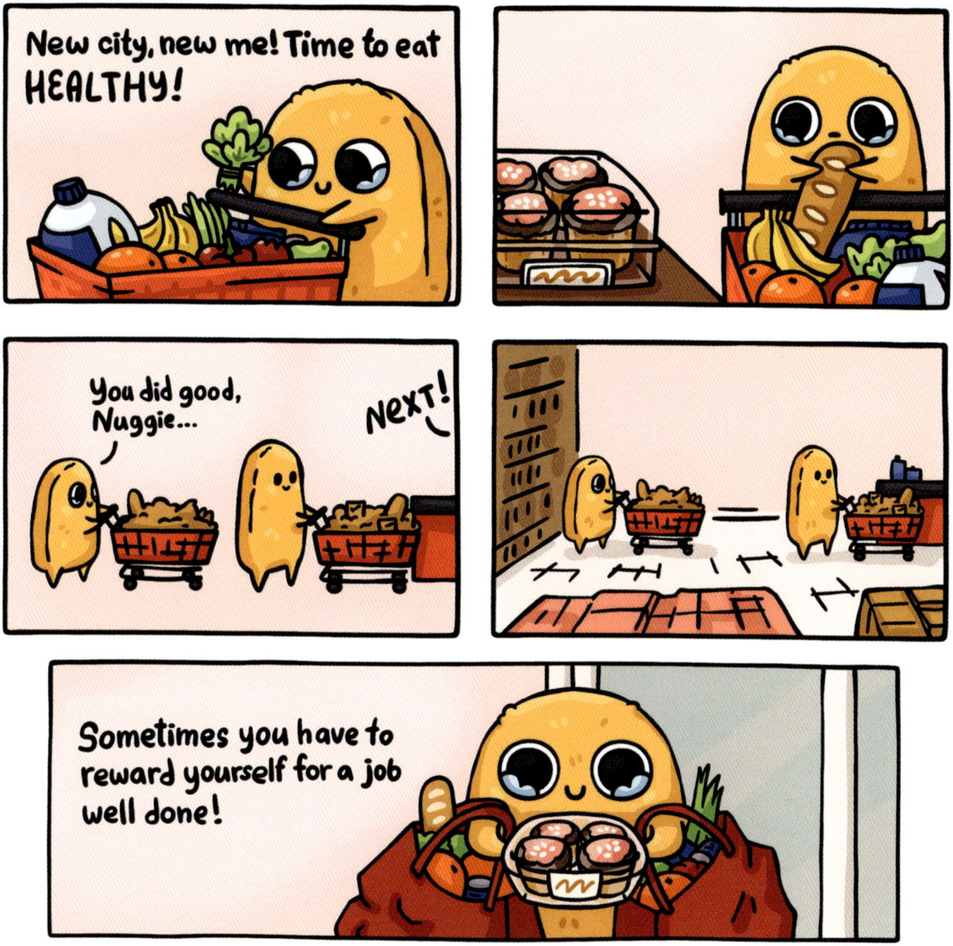
New city, new me! Time to eat HEALTHY!
You did good, Nuggie...
NEXT!
Sometimes you have to reward yourself for a job well done!

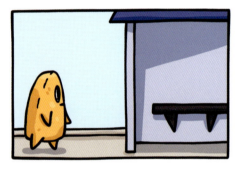

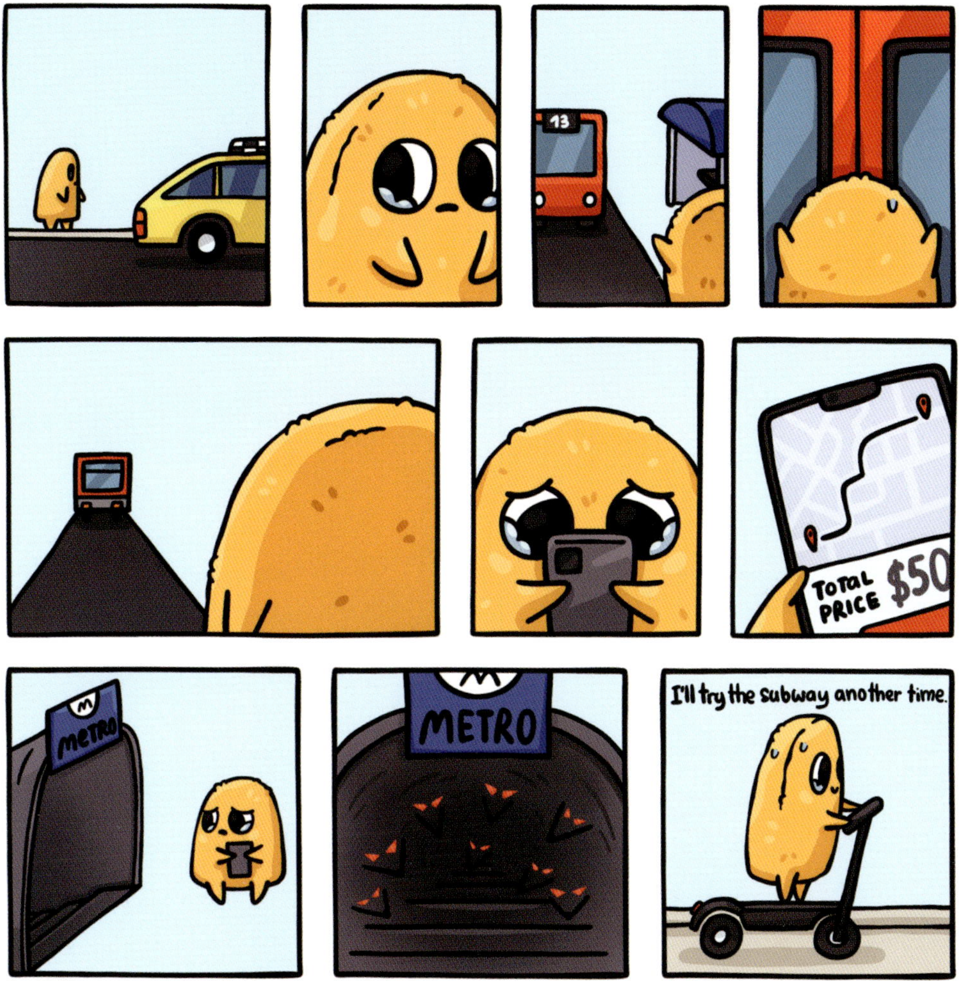
13
TOTAL PRICE $50
METRO
METRO
I'll try the subway another time.

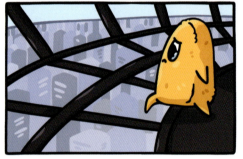
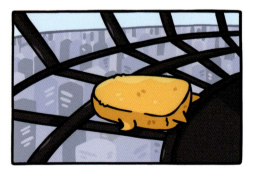

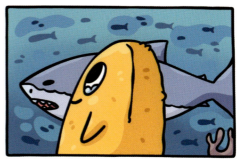

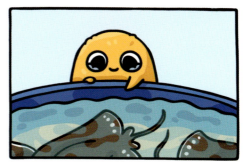

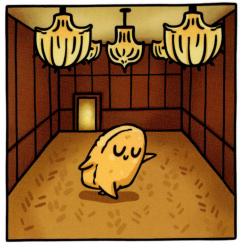

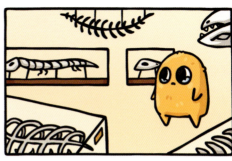

I bet they had some good snacks

What a fun city I live in

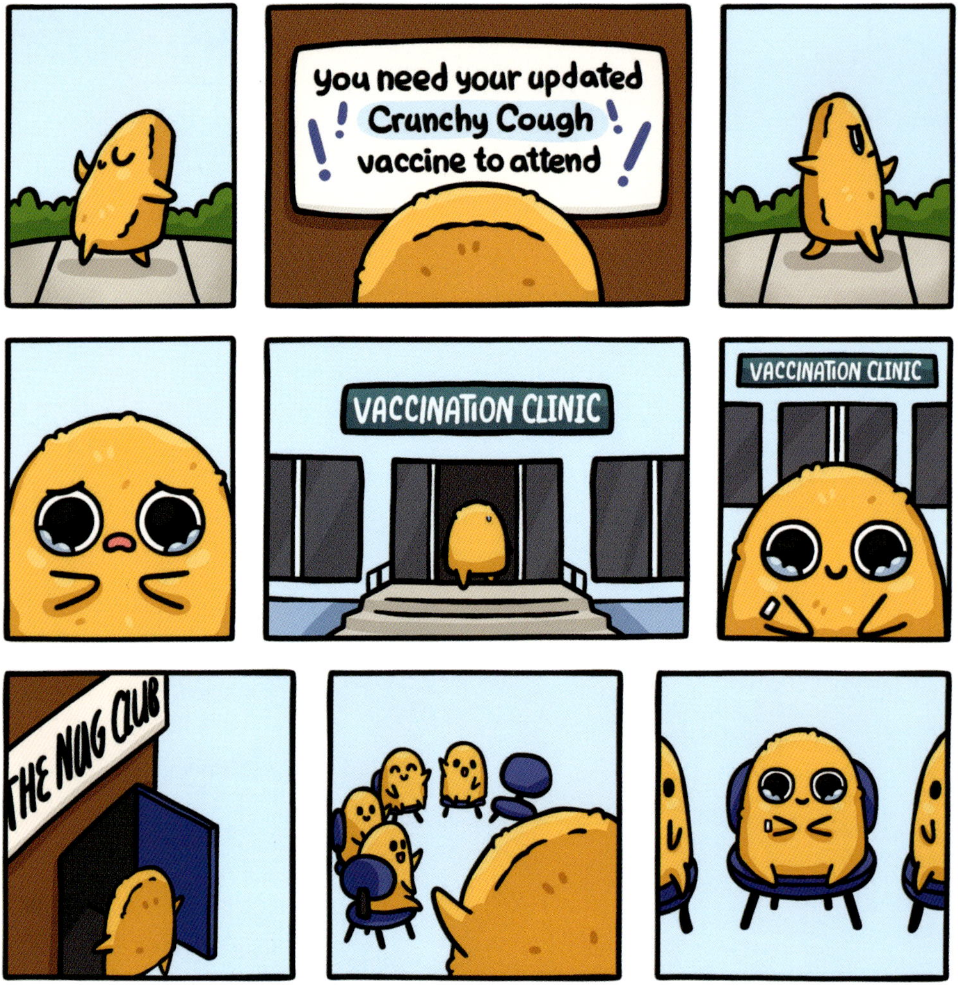
you need your updated Crunchy Cough vaccine to attend
! ! ! !
VACCINATION CLINIC
VACCINATION CLINIC
THE NUG CLUB

SAD NUGGIE'S RECIPE FOR ANXIETY

STEP 1:

Add one cup of overthinking.

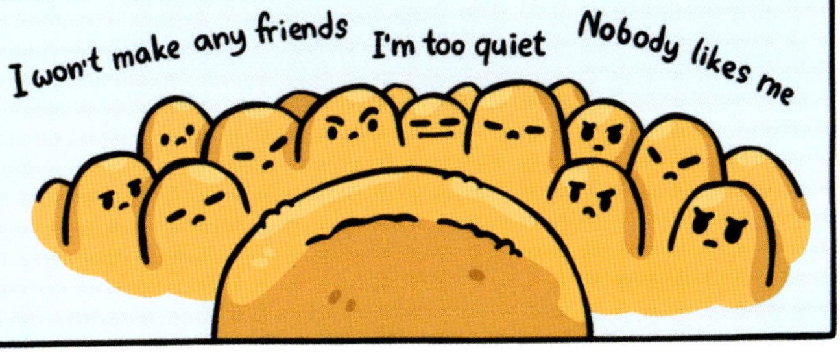
I won't make any friends
I'm too quiet
Nobody likes me

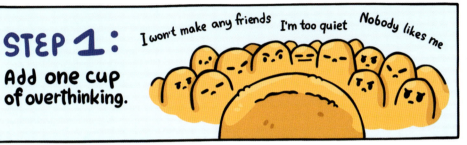

STEP 2:

Sprinkle in some regret.

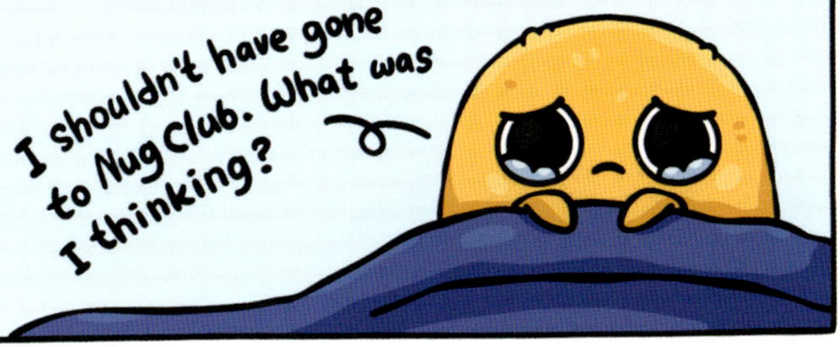
I shouldn't have gone to Nug Club. What was I thinking?

STEP 3:

Let marinate for 40-50 mins.

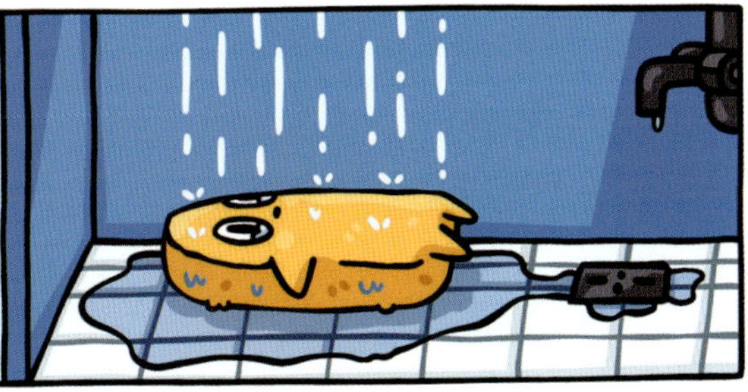

THERAPY SESSION 1

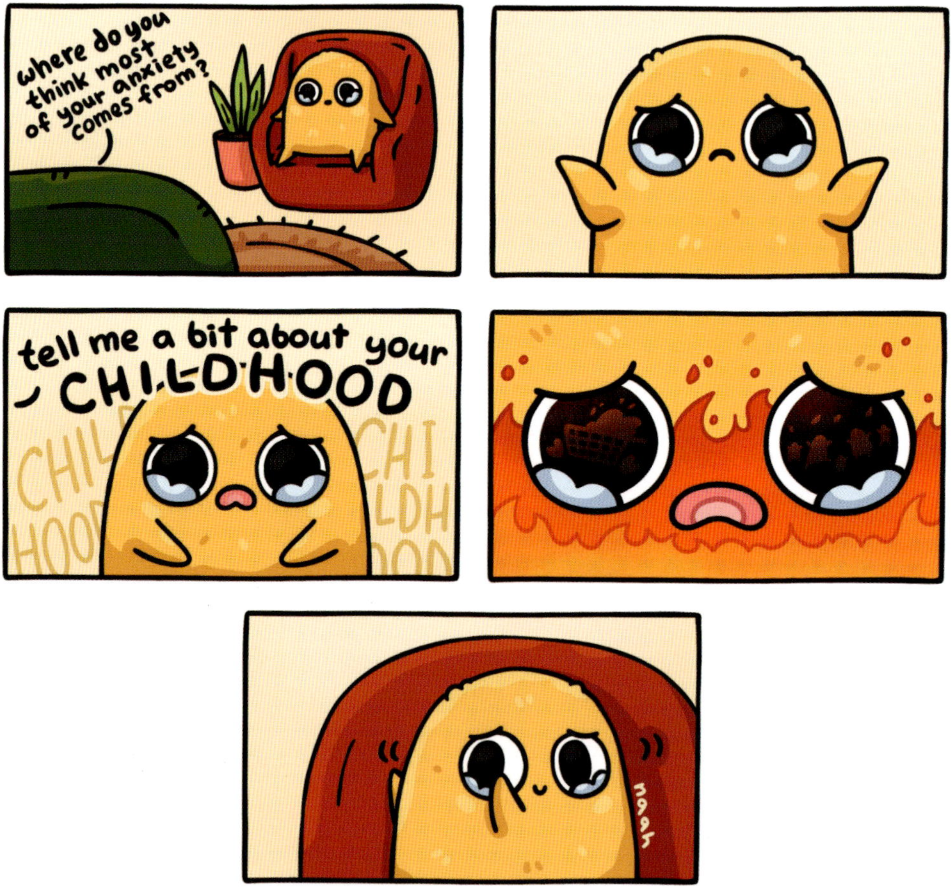
where do you think most of your anxiety comes from?
tell me a bit about your CHI·L·D·H·OOD
naah

CHAPTER 2

DOING MY
NUGGIE BEST

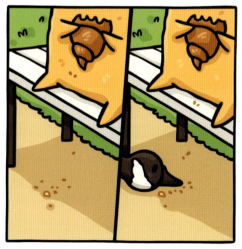

31

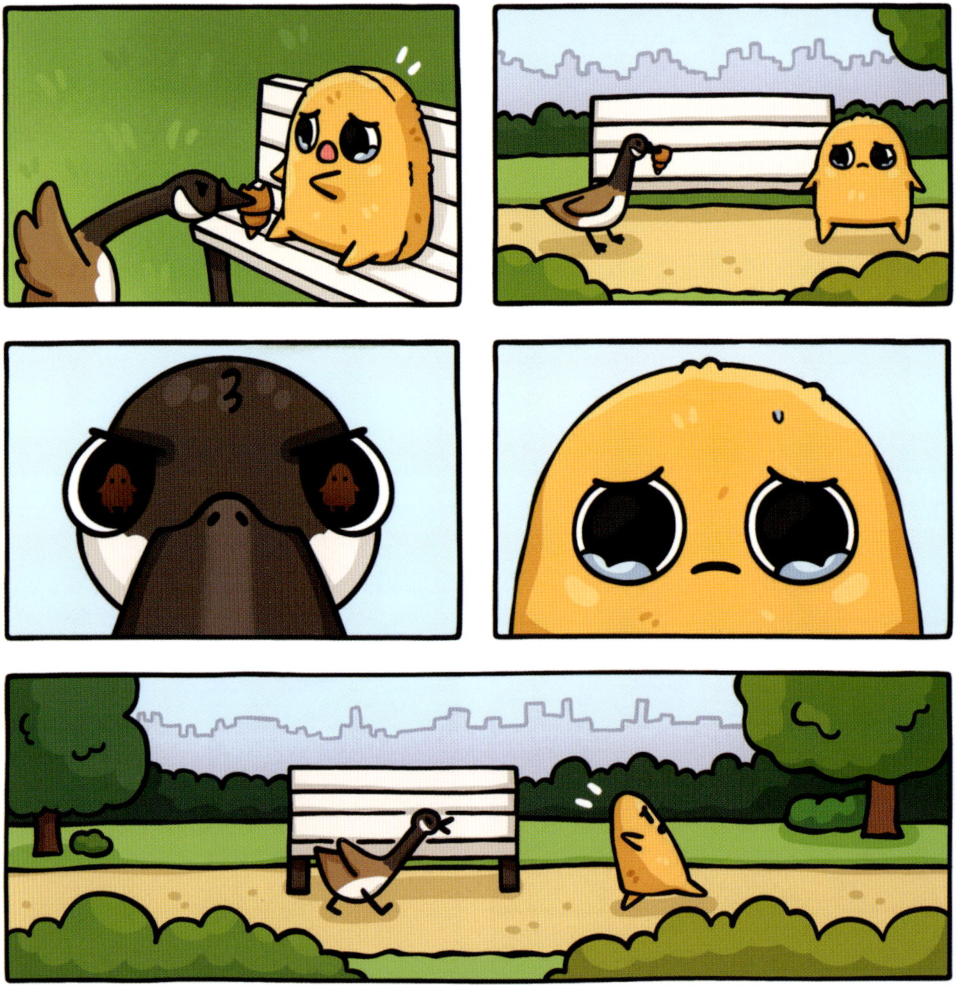

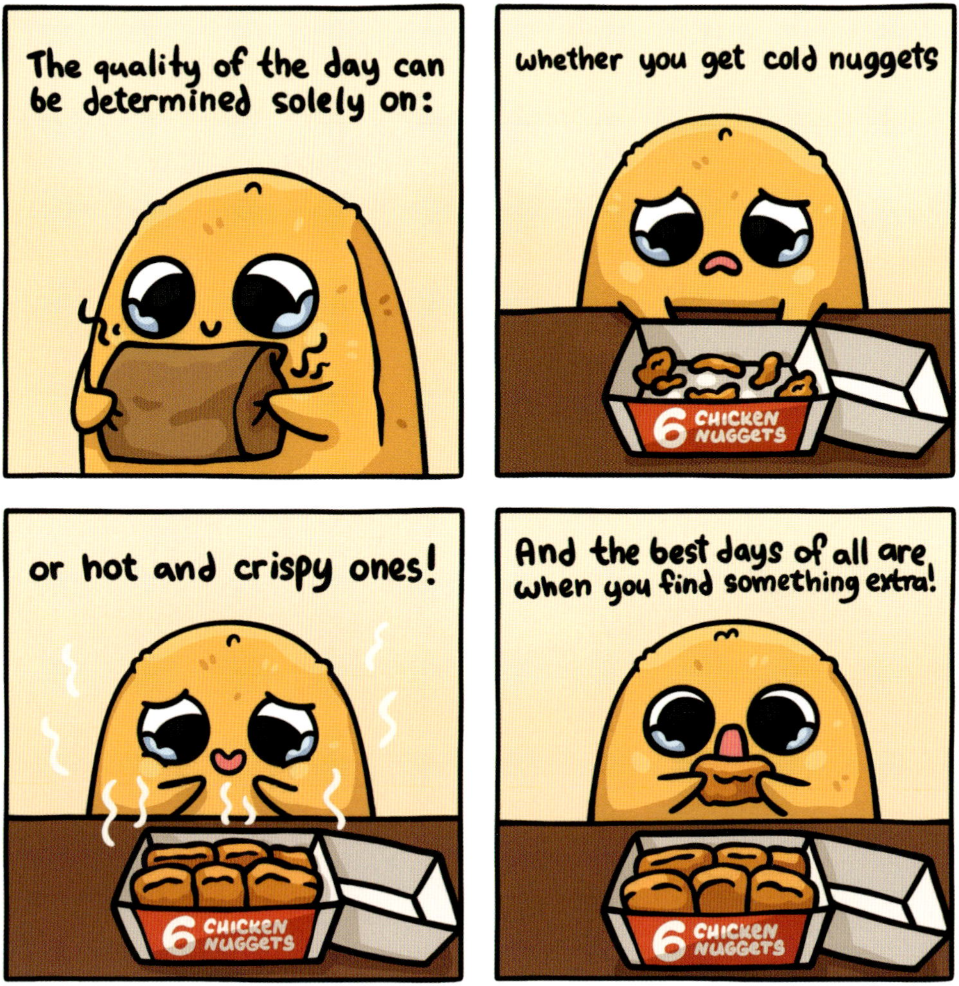
The quality of the day can be determined solely on:
whether you get cold nuggets
6 CHICKEN NUGGETS
or hot and crispy ones!
6 CHICKEN NUGGETS
And the best days of all are when you find something extra!
6 CHICKEN NUGGETS

maybe I need a little retail therapy...

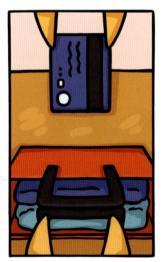

MOBILE BANK

CURRENT balance
$0.00

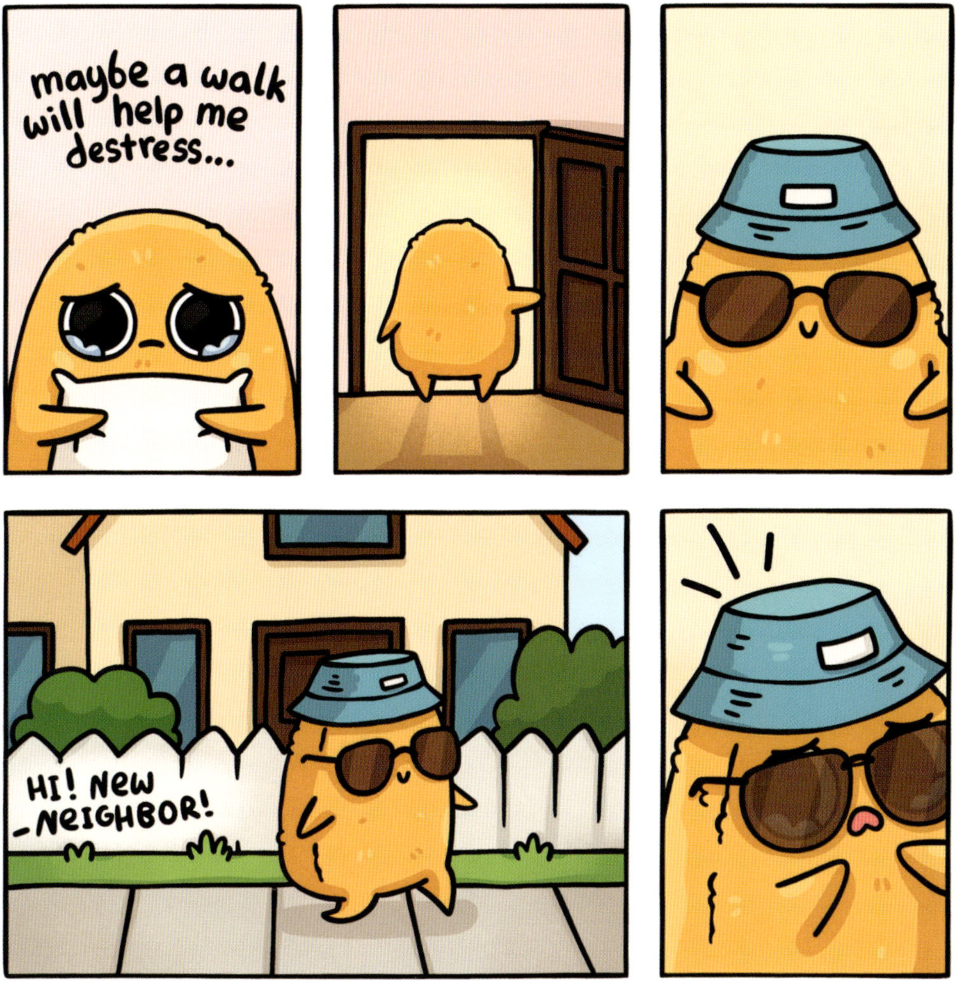
maybe a walk will help me destress...
HI! New NEIGHBOR!

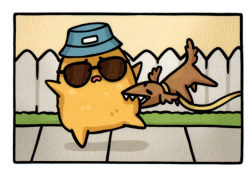

WATCH WHERE YOU'RE GOING!

WALKS ARE TOO PEOPLE-Y

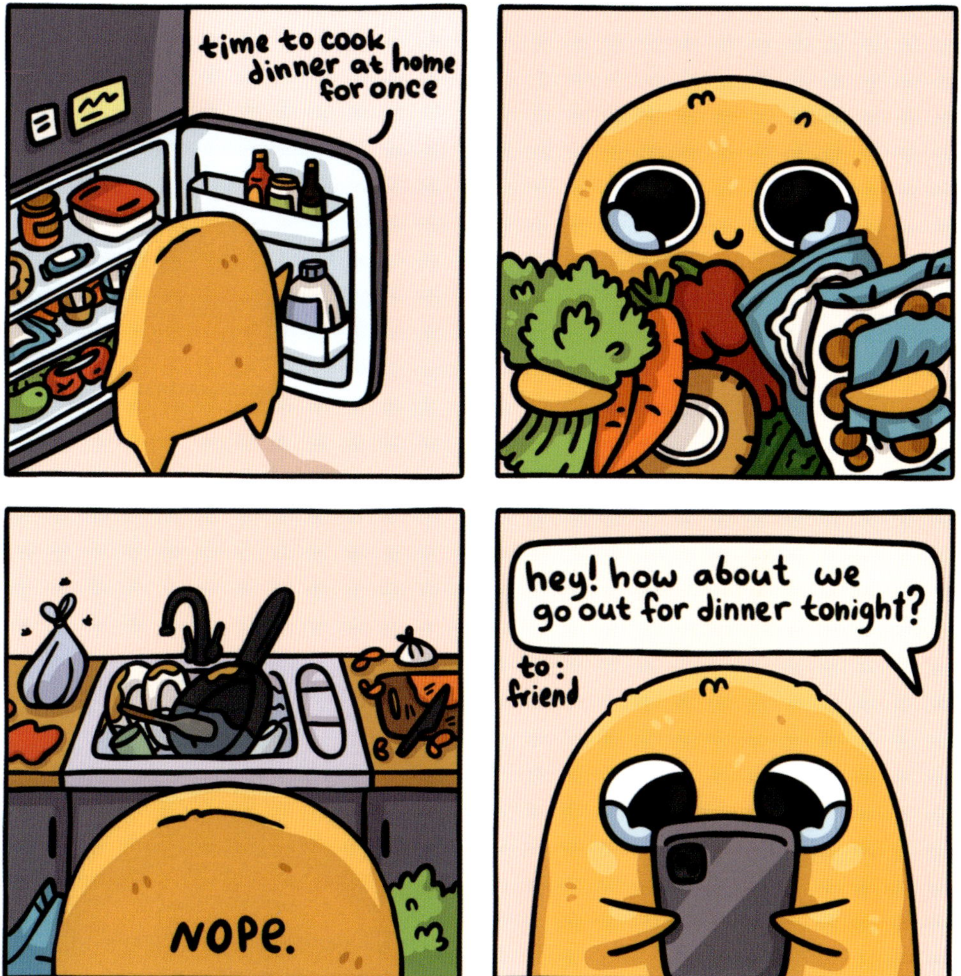
time to cook dinner at home for once
NOPE.
hey! how about we go out for dinner tonight?
to: friend

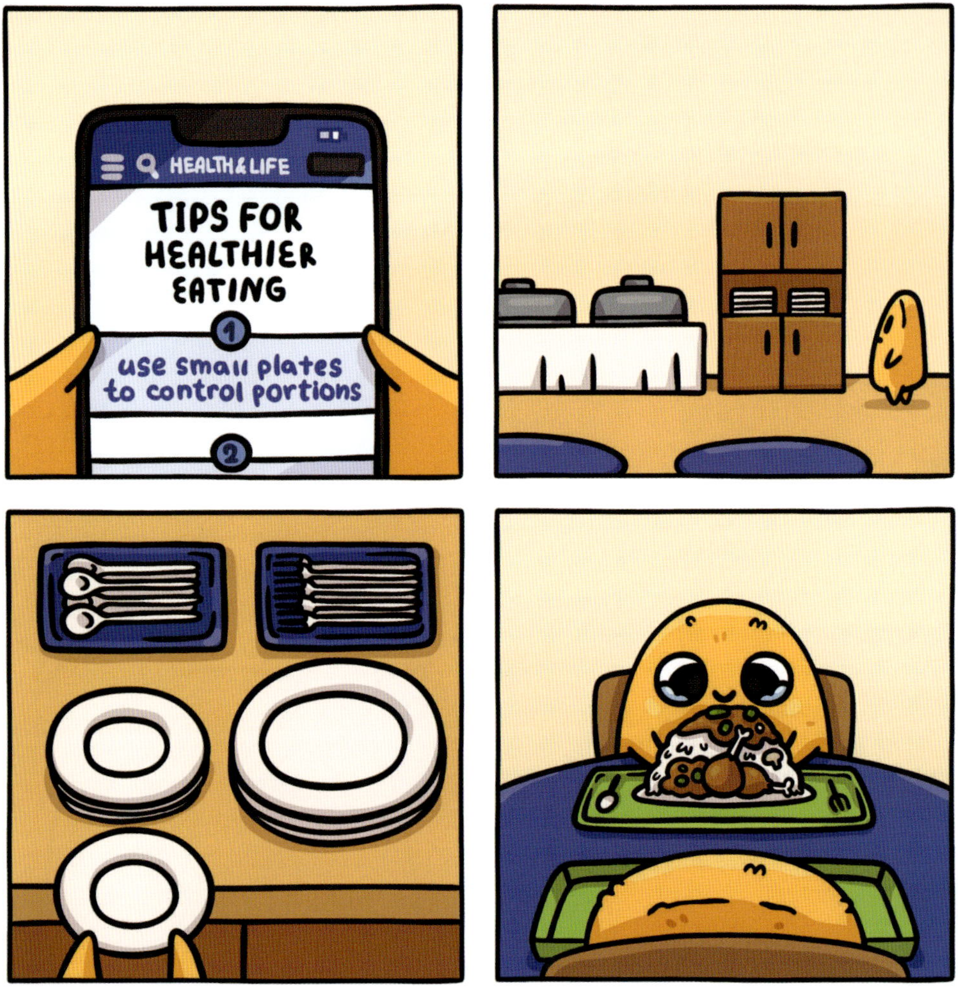
HEALTH & LIFE
TIPS FOR HEALTHIER EATING
1
use small plates to control portions
2

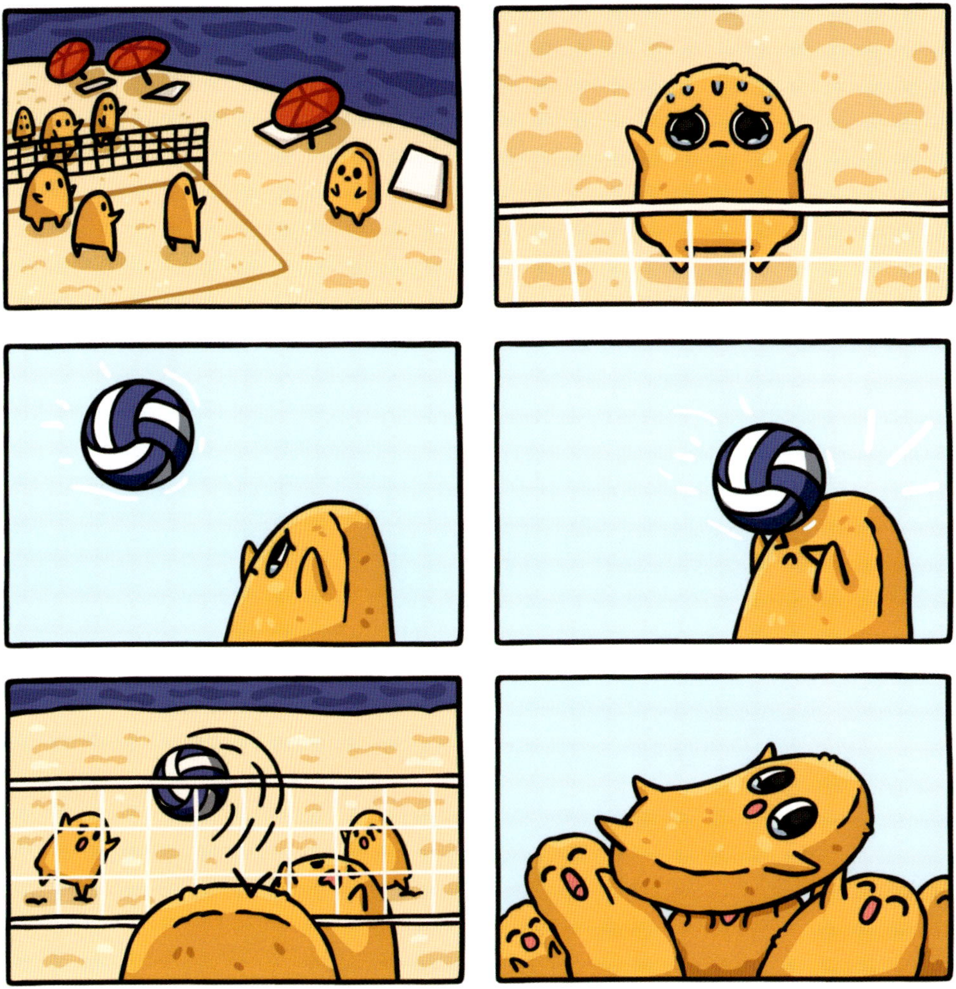

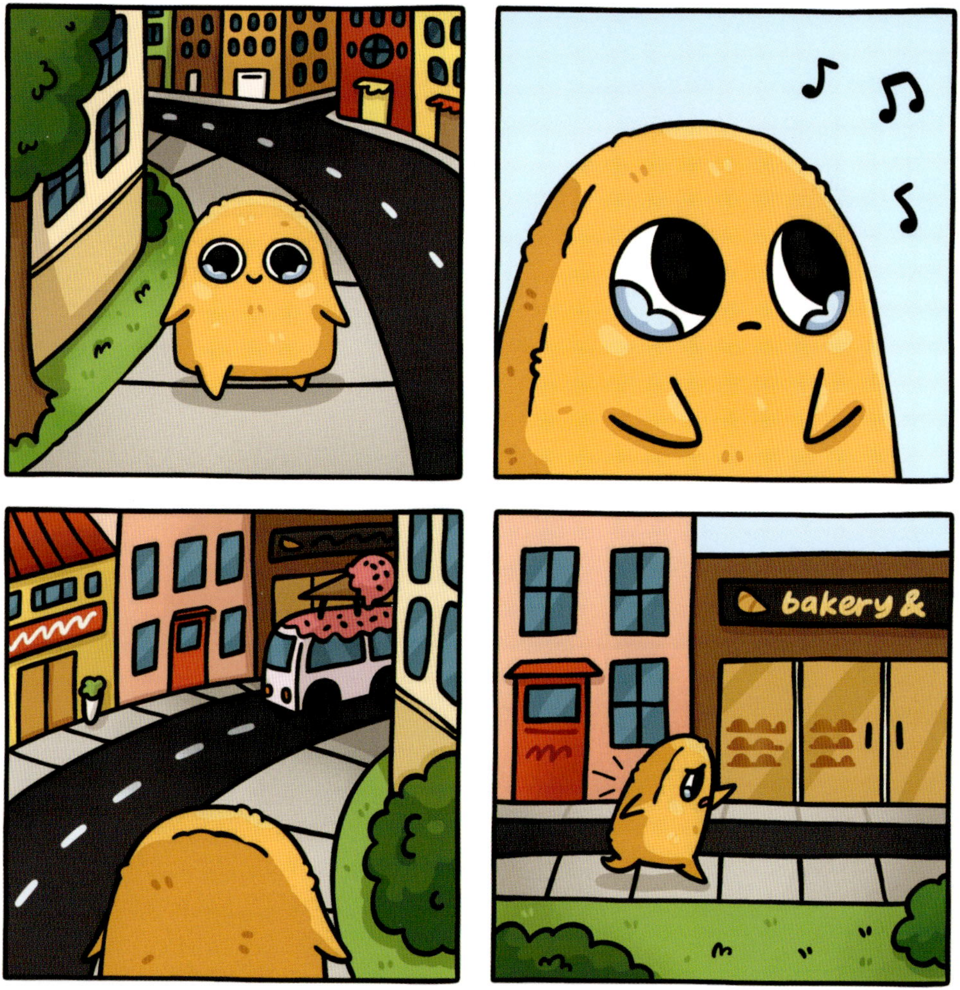
bakery &

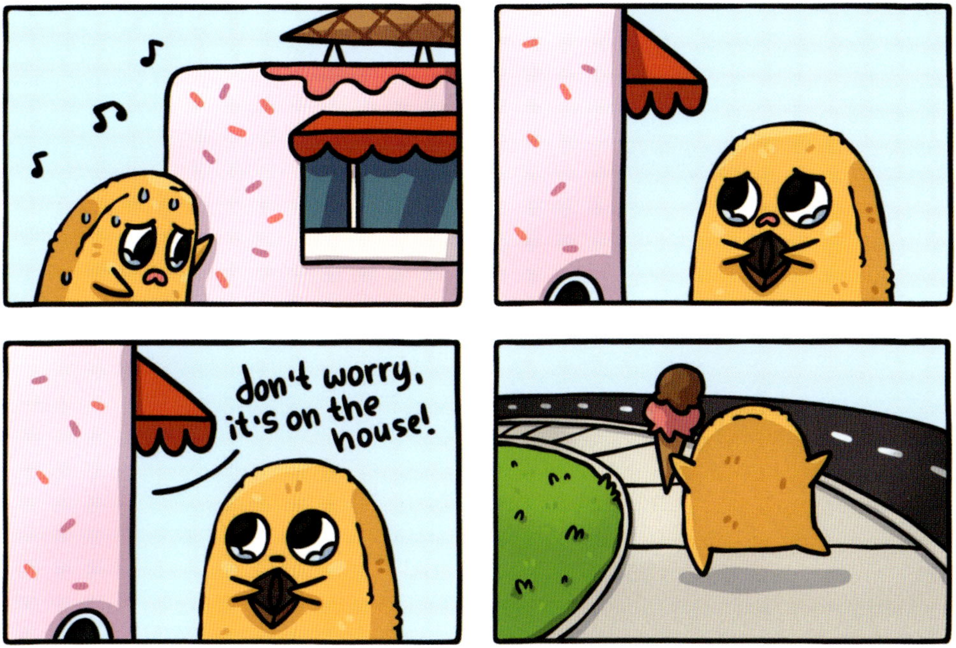
don't worry, it's on the house!

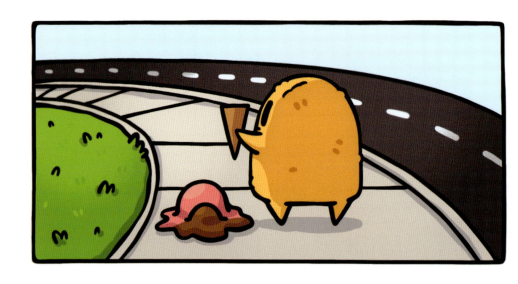

SOMETIMES YOU NEED TO PAMPER YOURSELF LIKE A NUGGET KING.

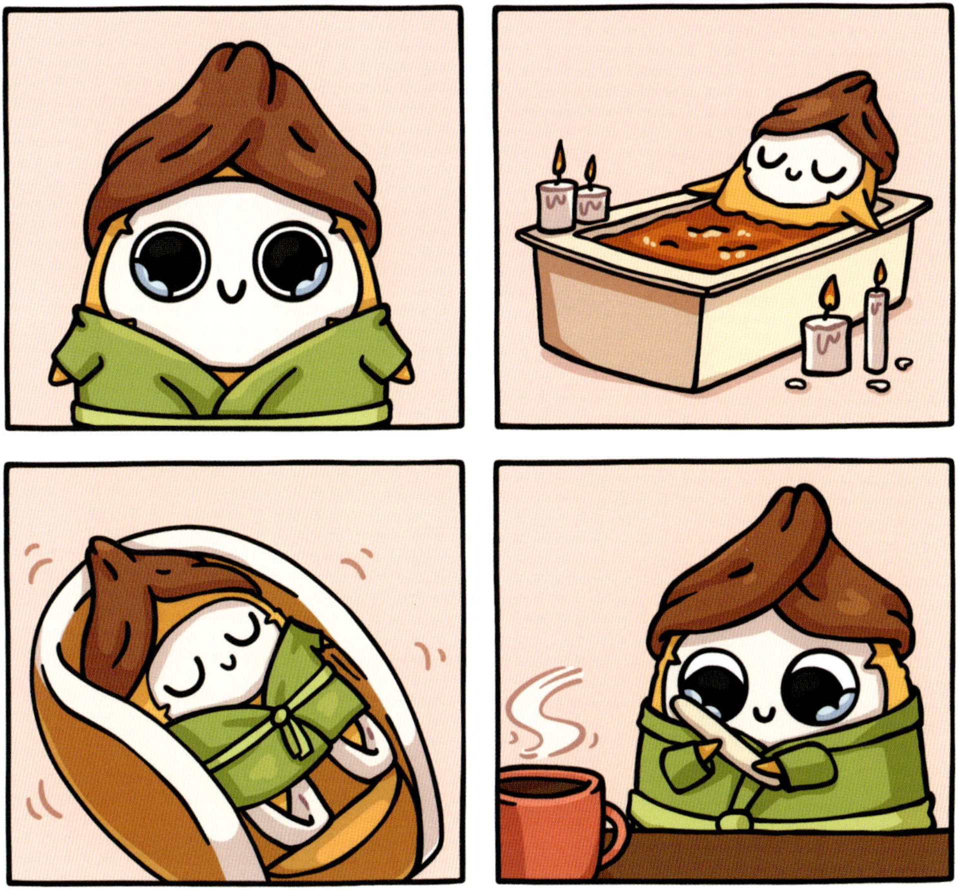

THERAPY SESSION 2

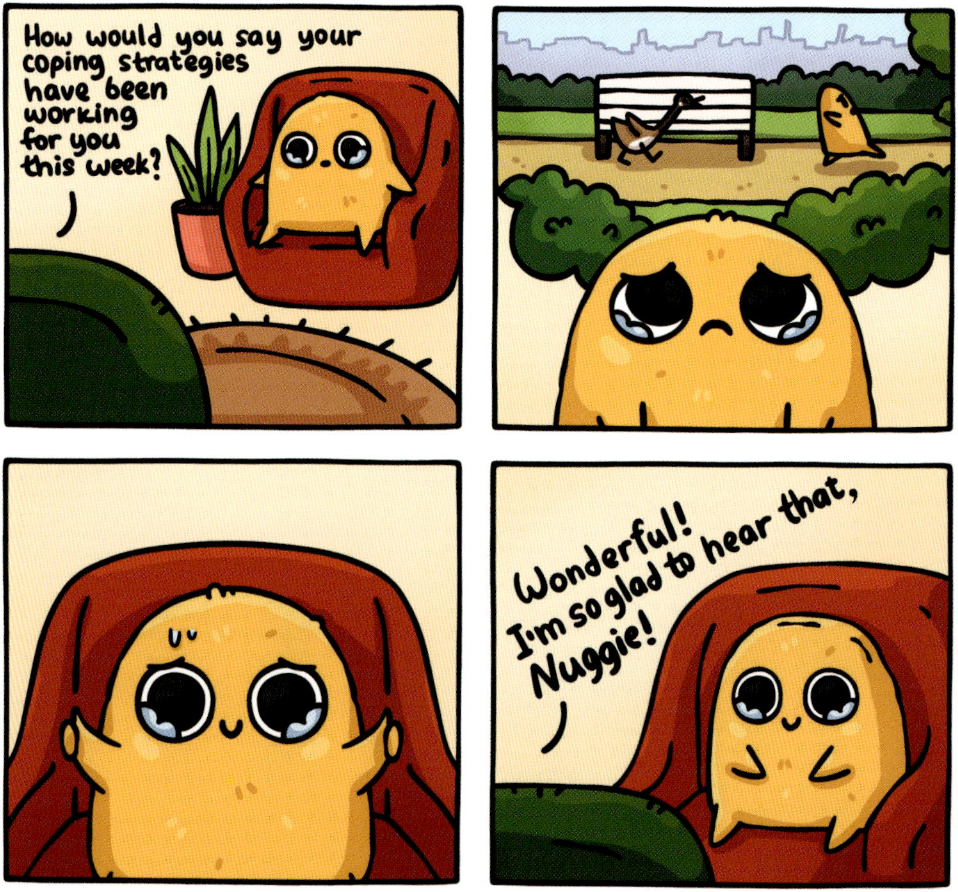
How would you say your coping strategies have been working for you this week?
Wonderful! I'm so glad to hear that, Nuggie!

CHAPTER 3

A BIG ADVENTURE

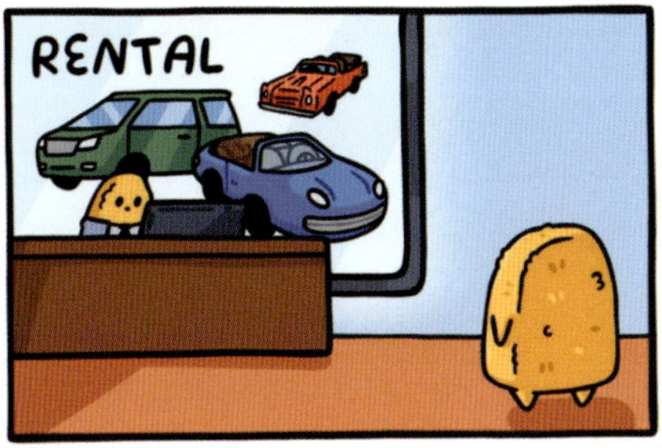
RENTAL
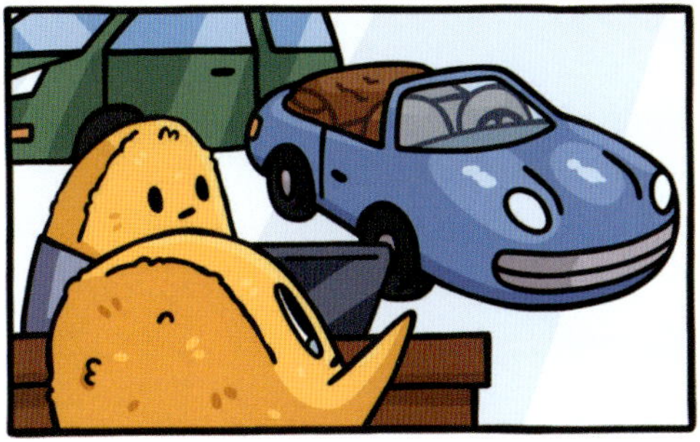
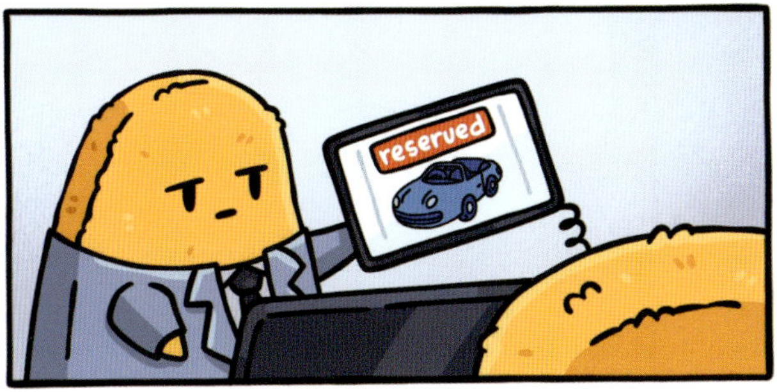
reserved
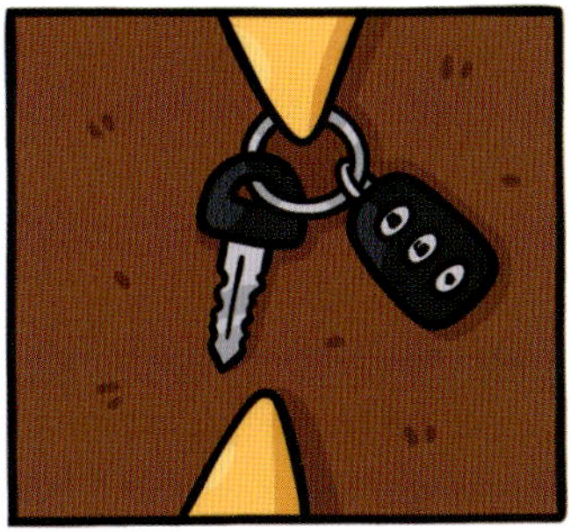
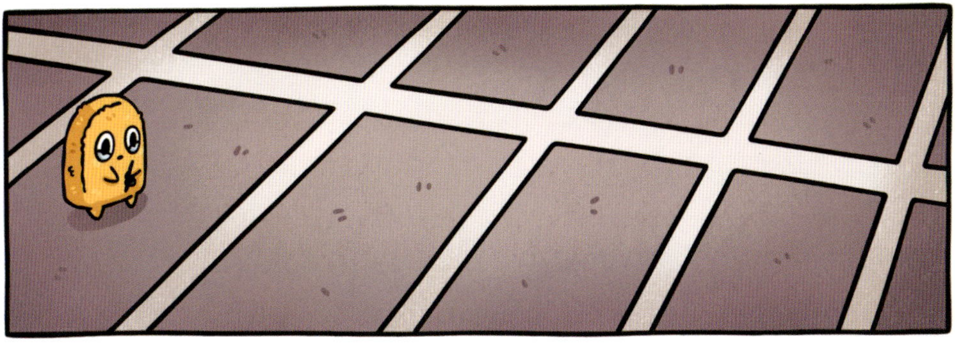

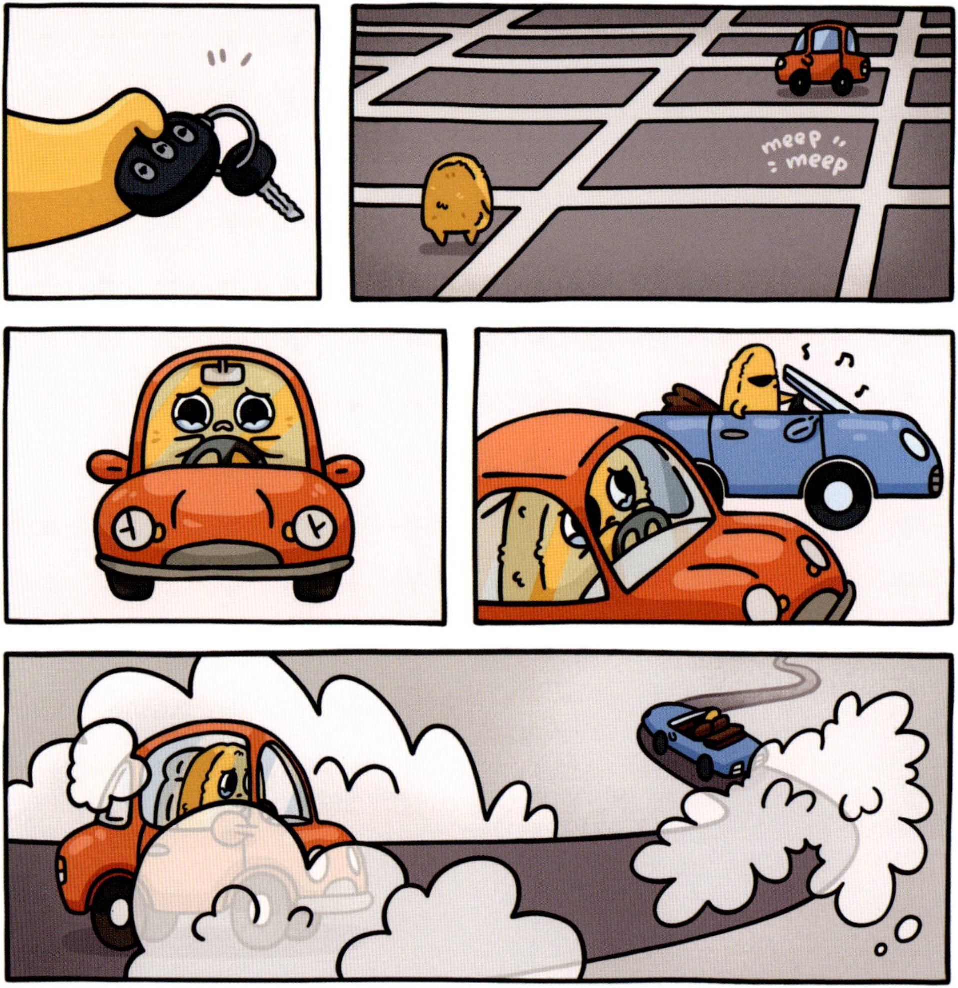
meep meep

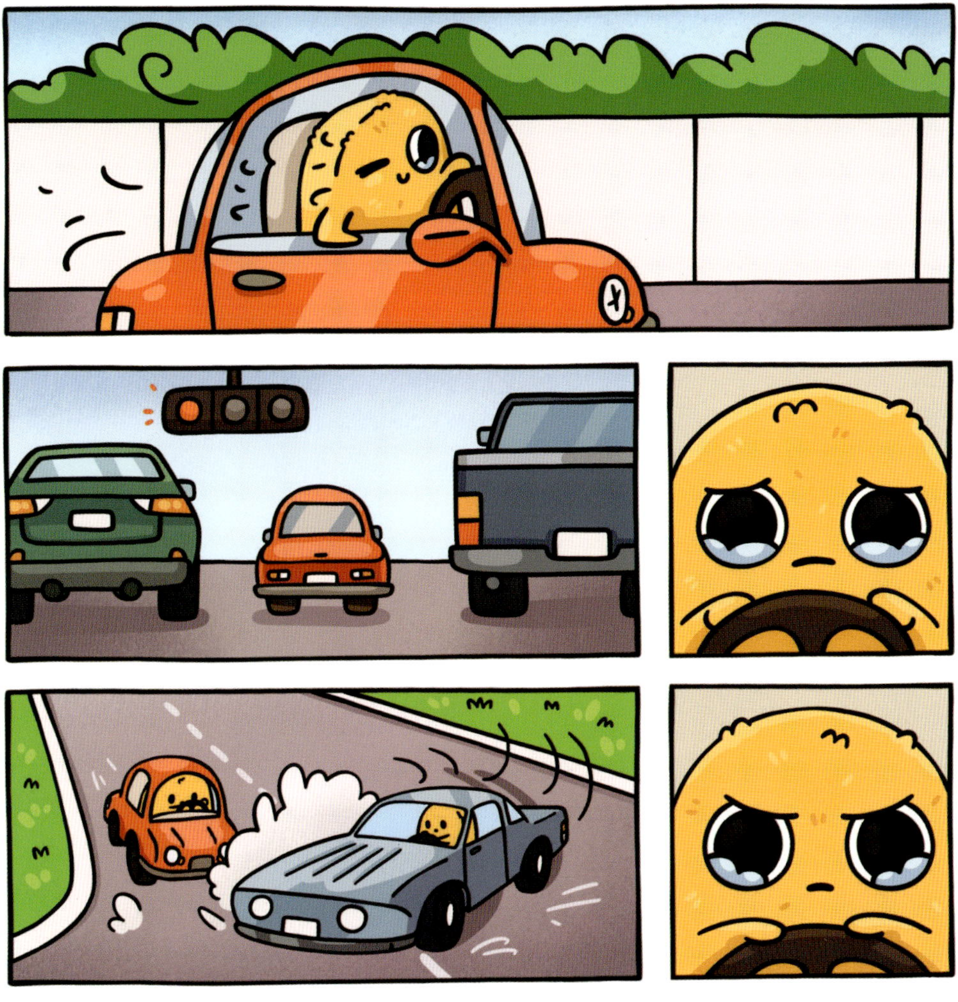

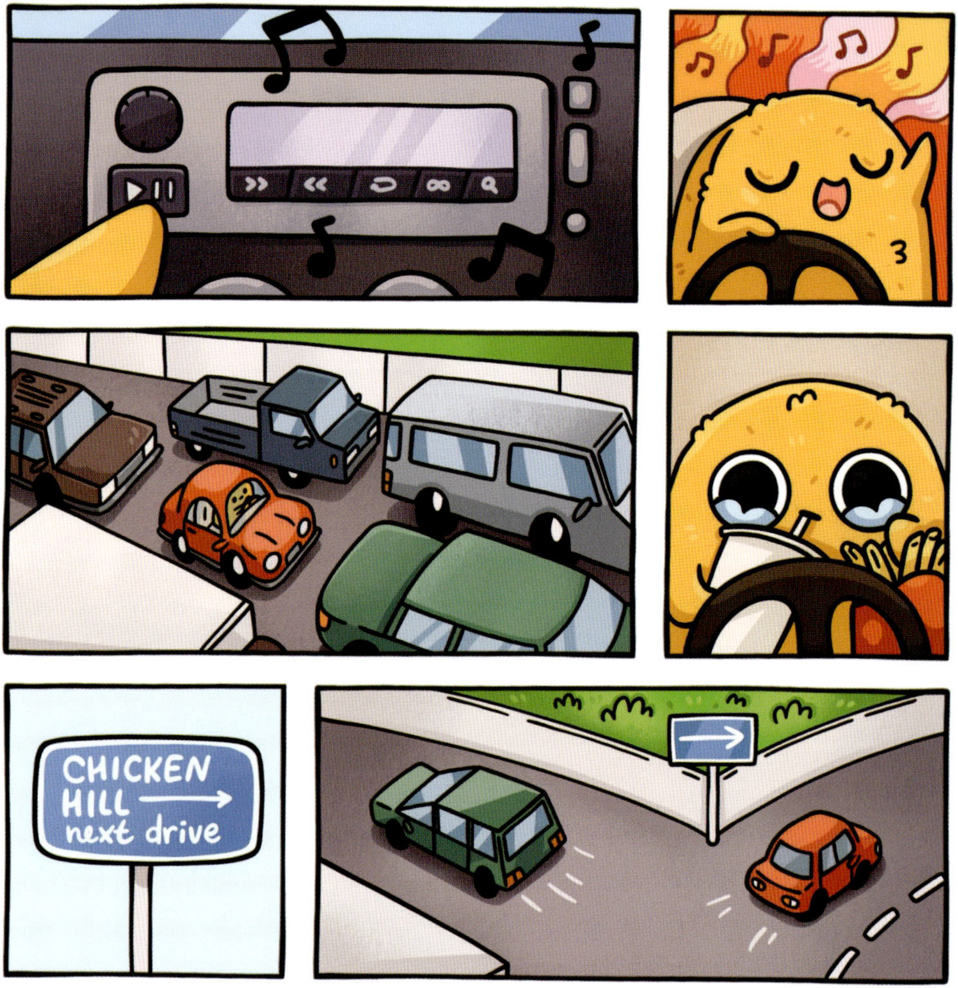
CHICKEN HILL
next drive

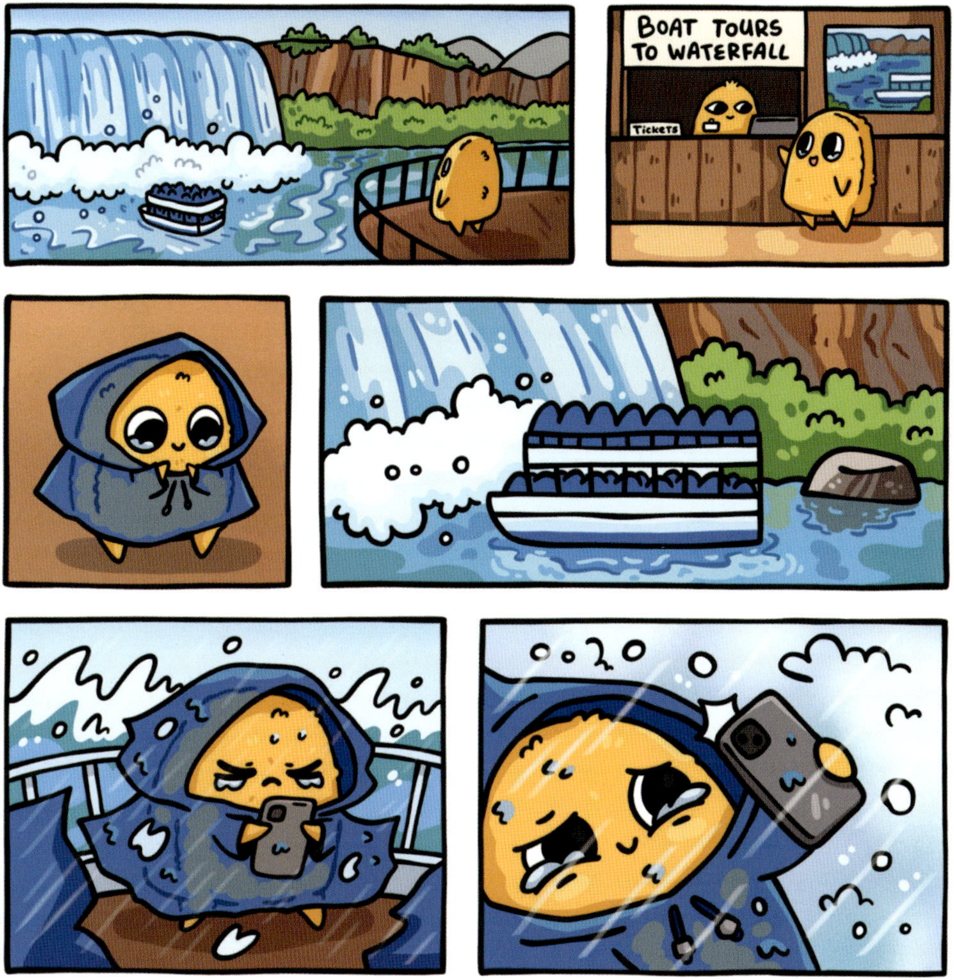
BOAT TOURS
TO WATERFALL
Tickets

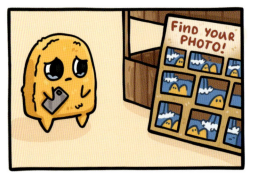

FIND YOUR PHOTO!

a ton of $$$

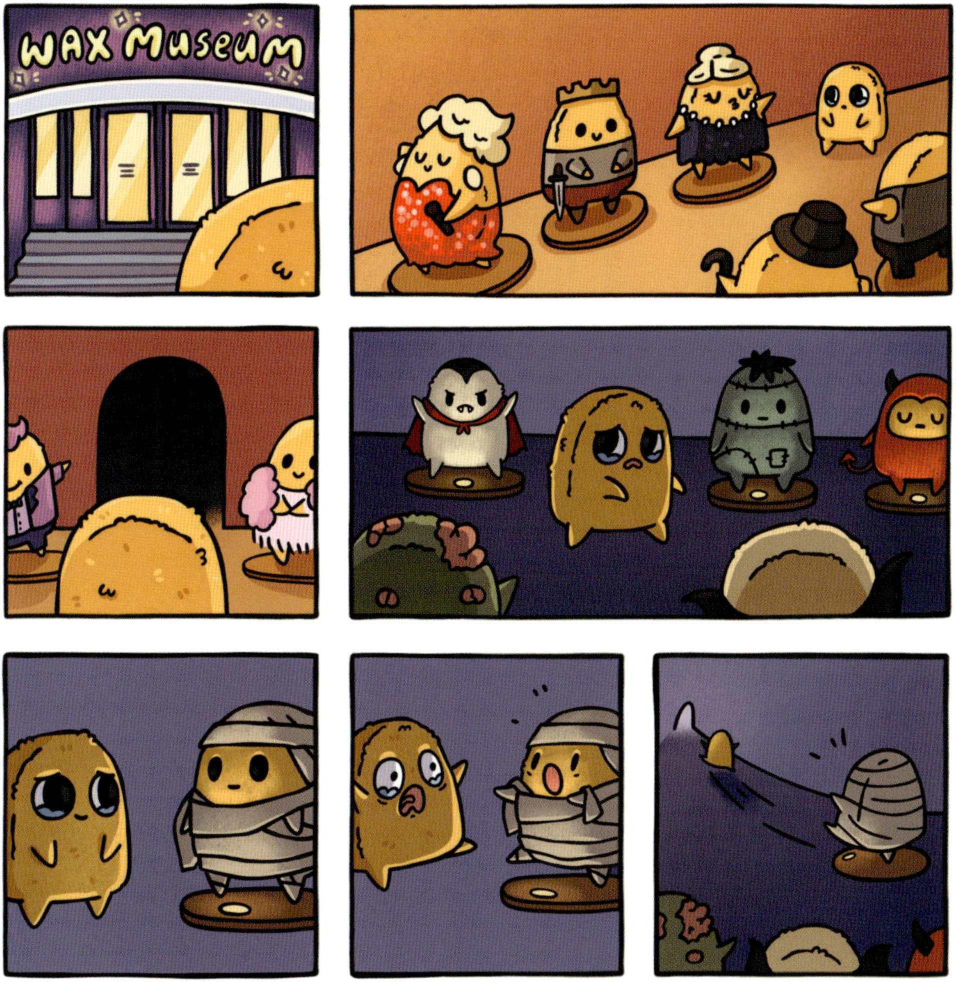
WAX MUSEUM

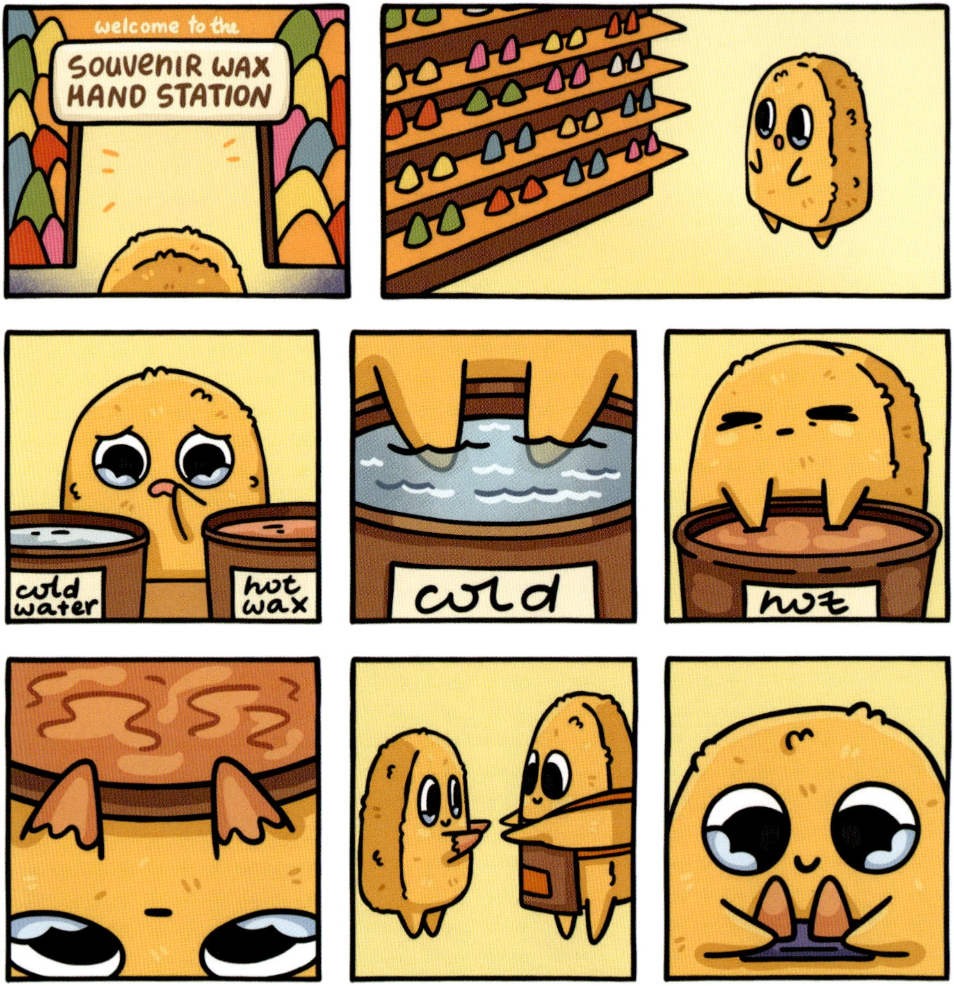
welcome to the
SOUVENIR WAX HAND STATION
cold water
hot wax
cold
hot

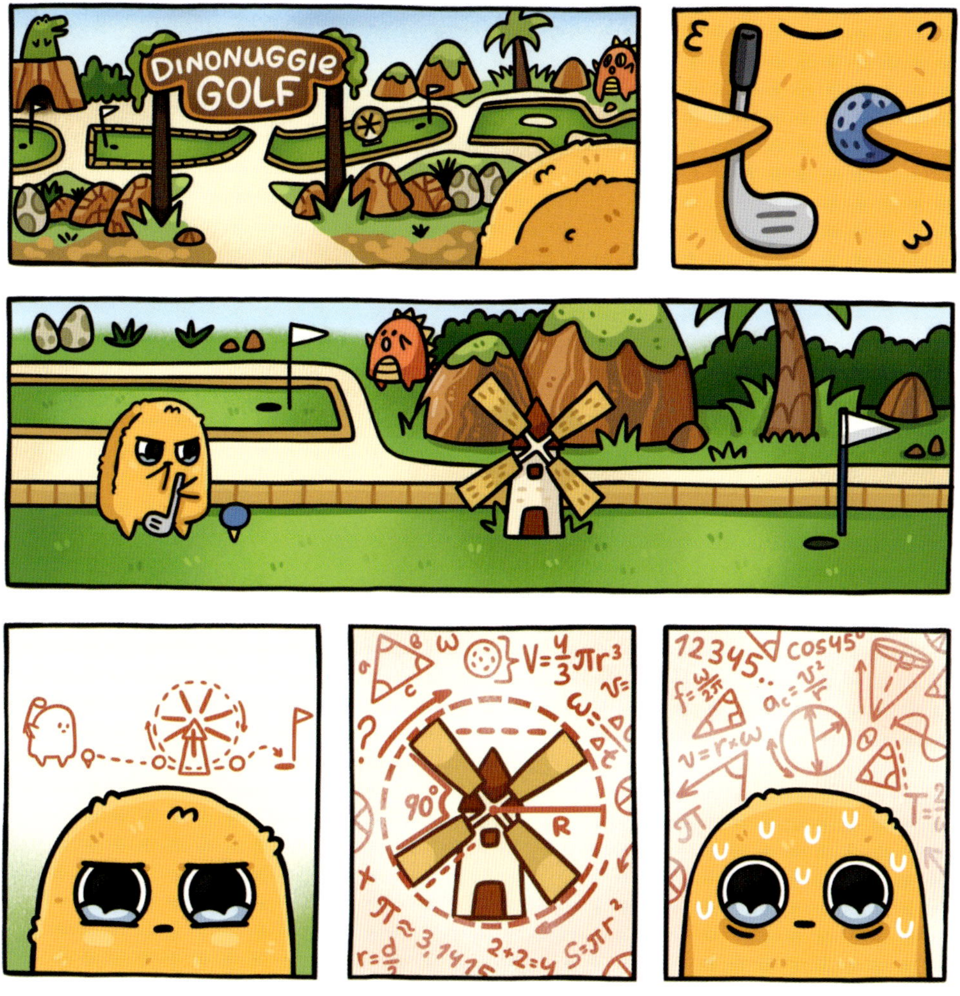
DINONUGGIE GOLF
V=4/3πr³
ω=Δθ/Δt
90°
R
π≈3.1415
r=d/2
2+2=4
S=πr²
12345..
cos45°
f=ω/2π
aᶜ=v²/r
v=r×ω

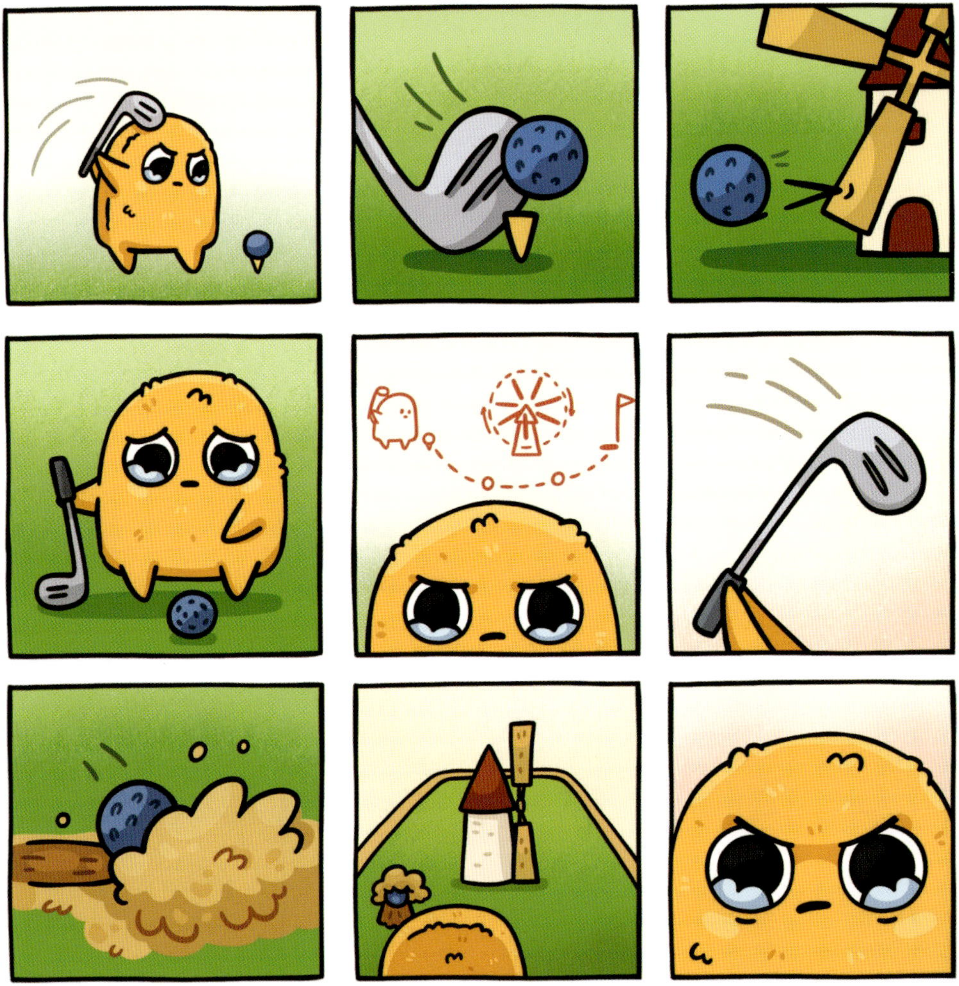

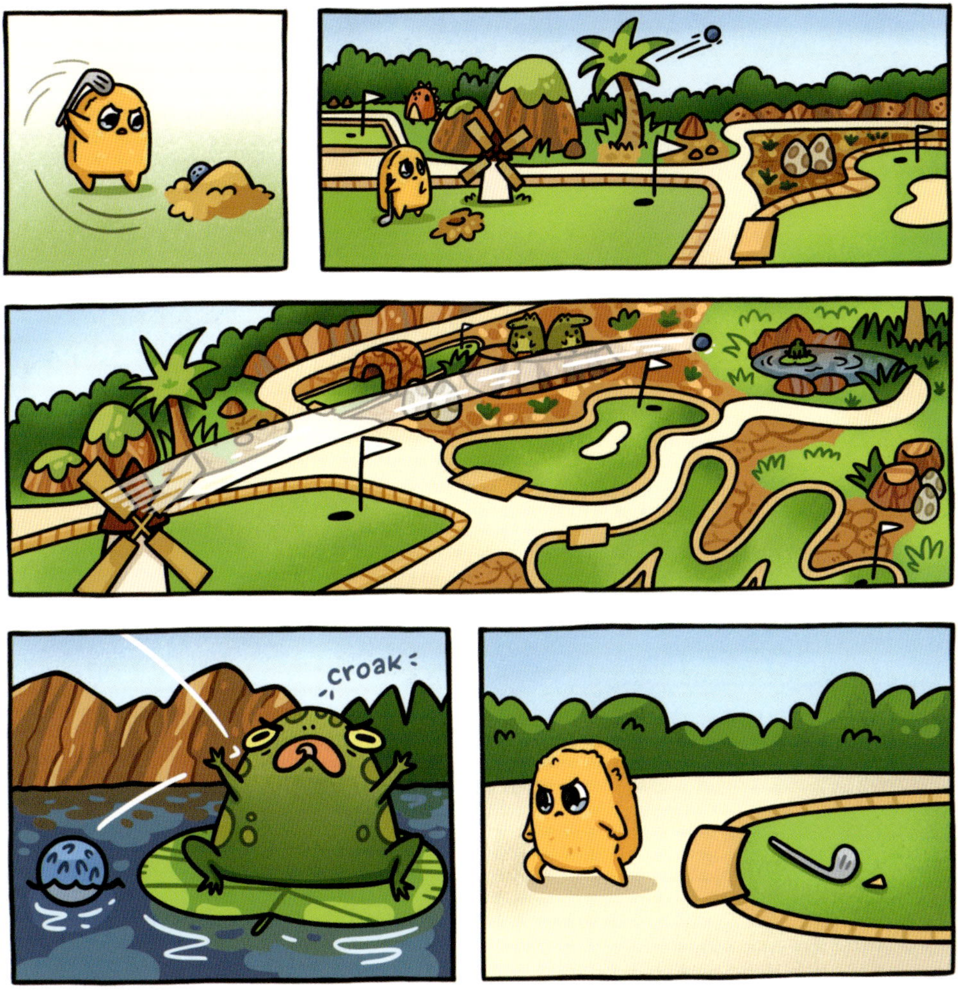
croak

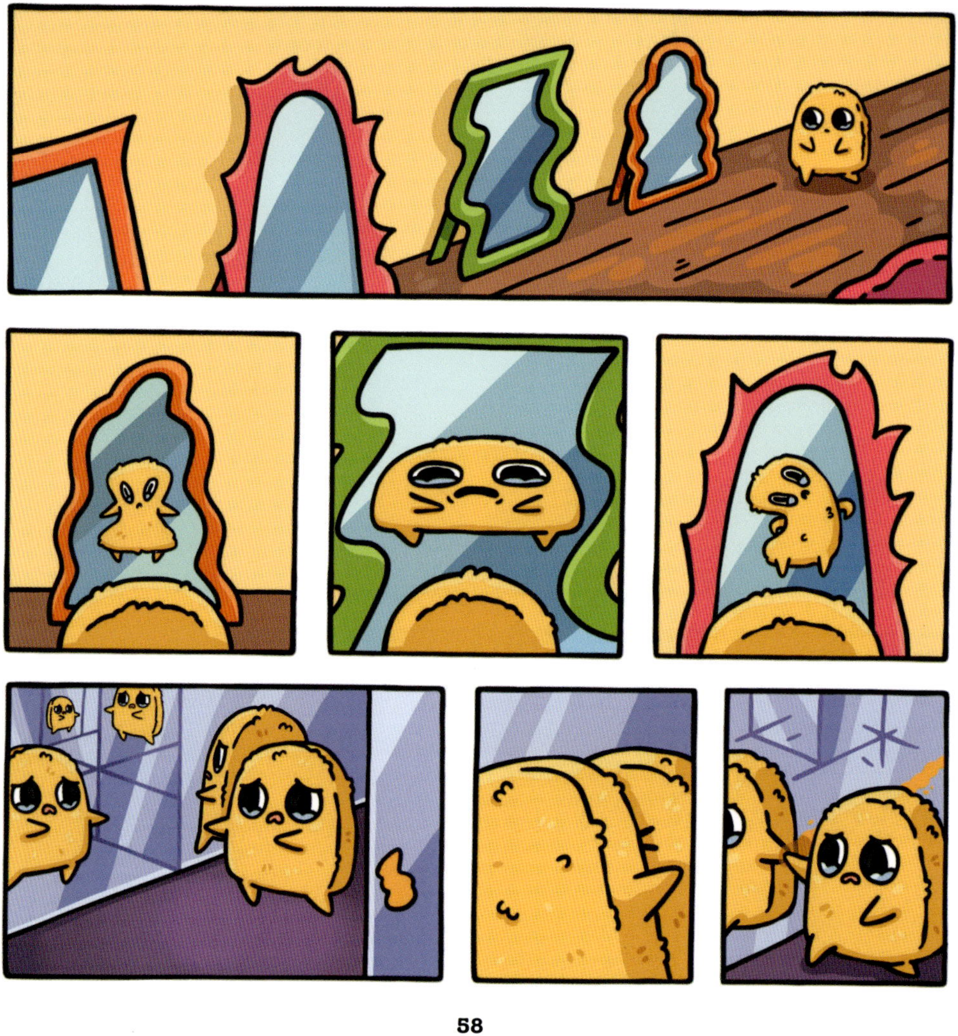

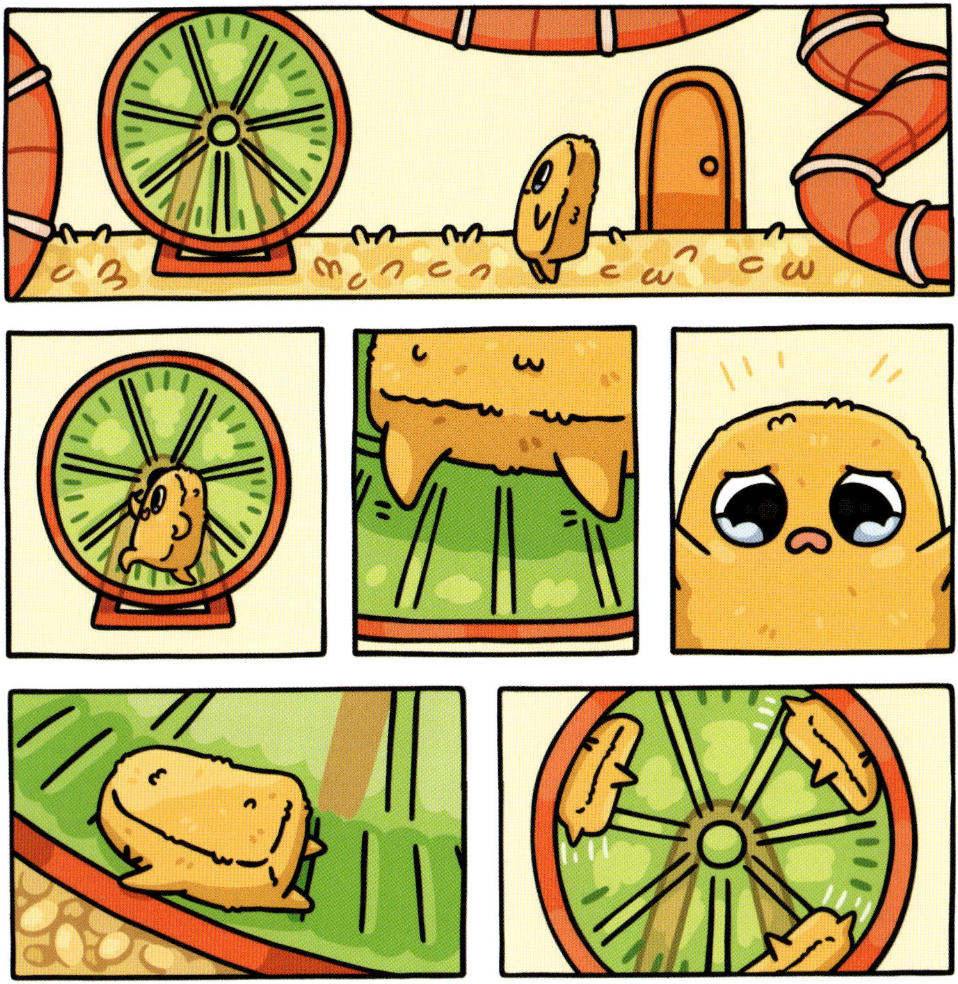

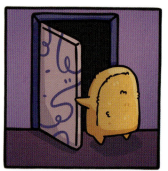

boo!

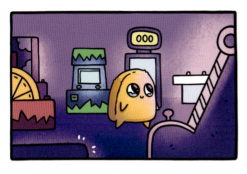

PLEASE insert the coin
LET'S PLAY
JACKPOT!
JACKPOT!

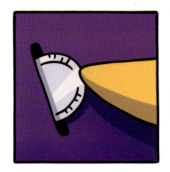

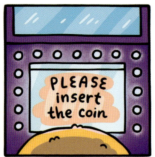

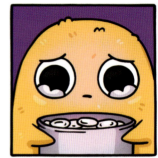

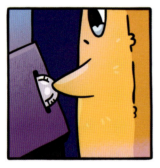

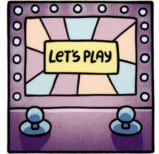

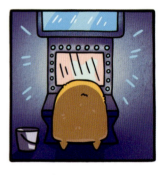

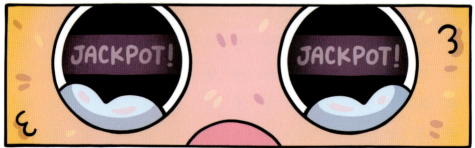

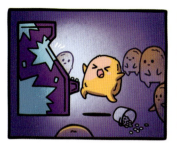

bzzzz...

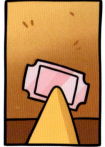

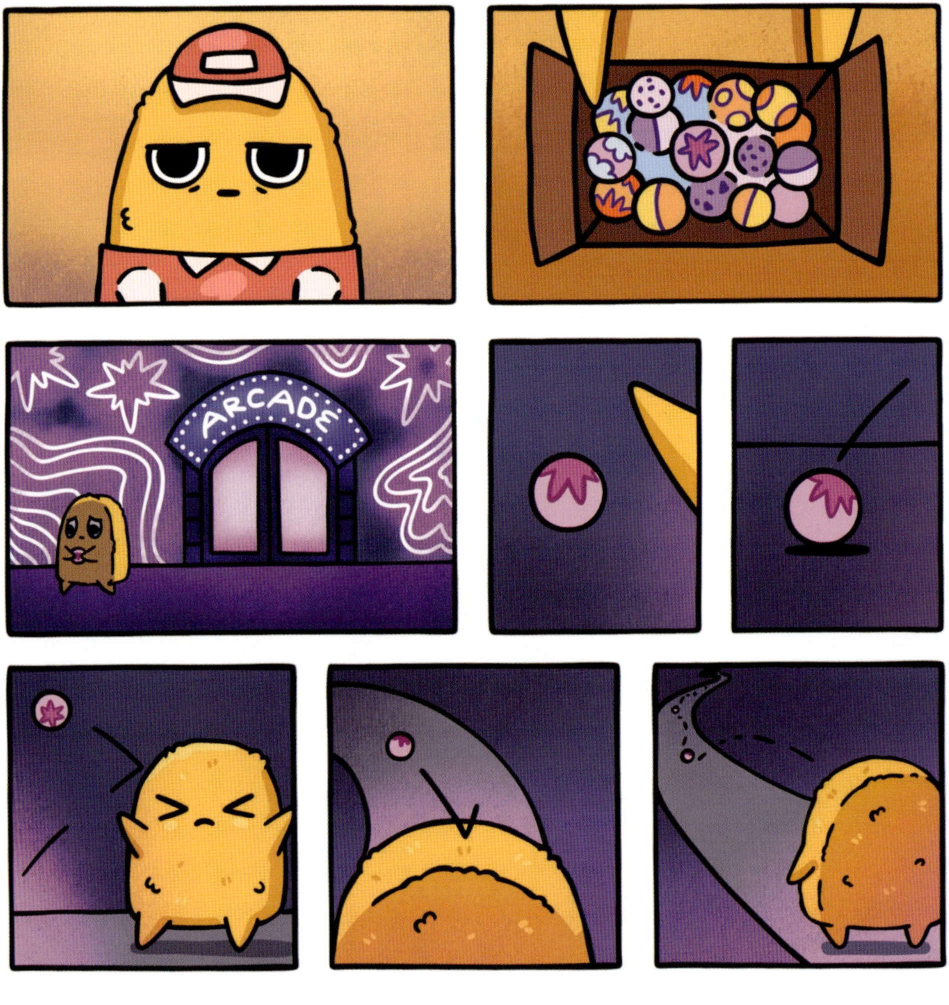
ARCADE

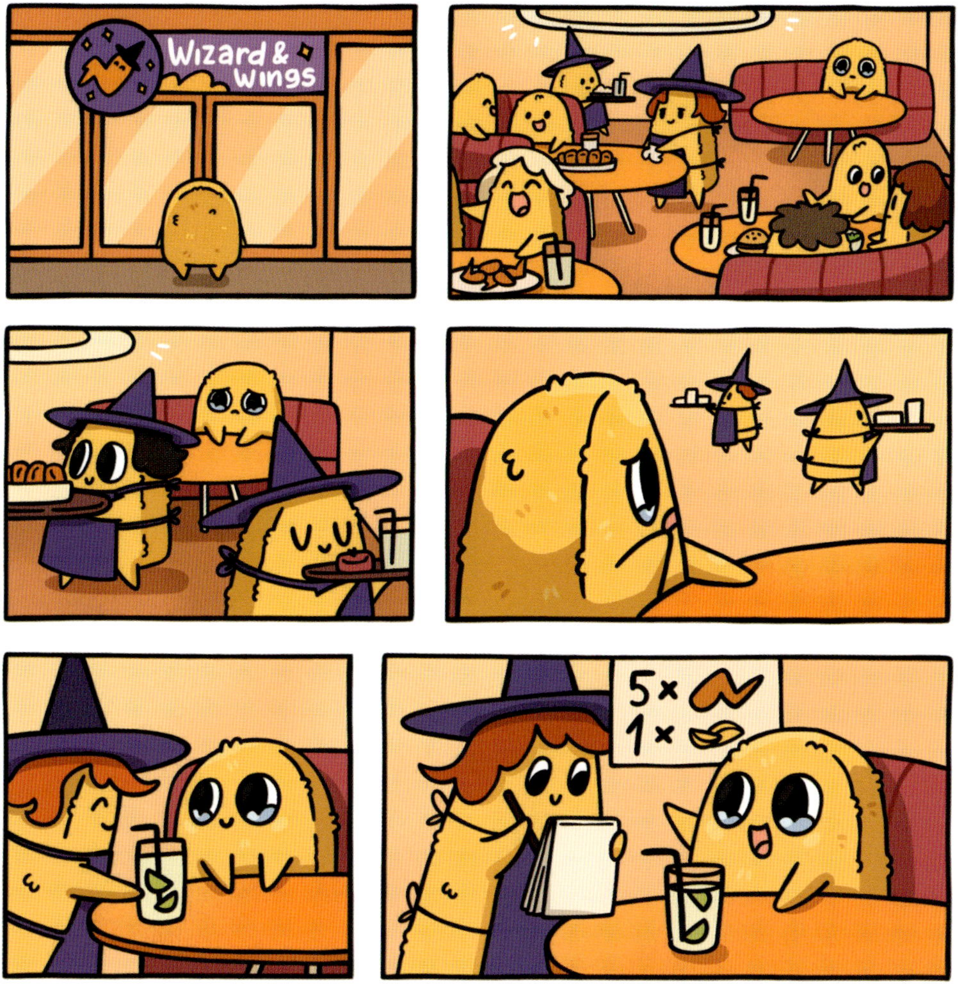
Wizard &
Wings
5 ×
1 ×

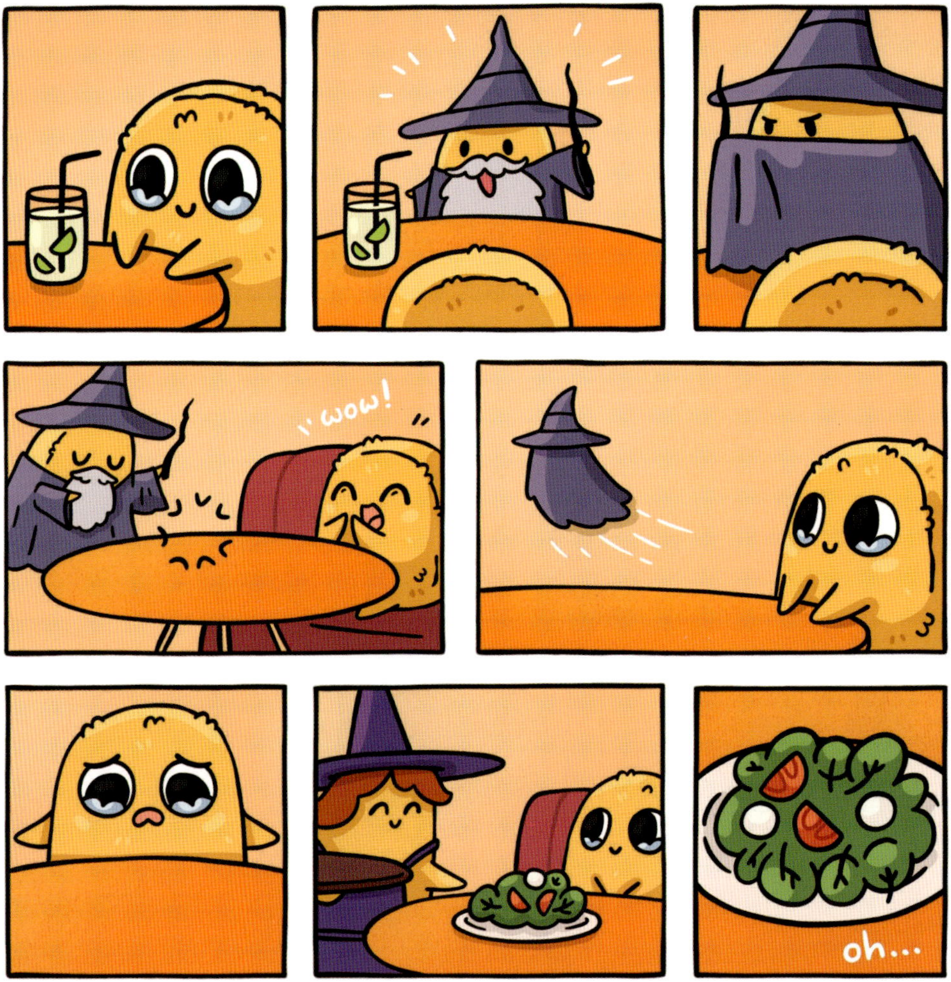
wow!
oh...

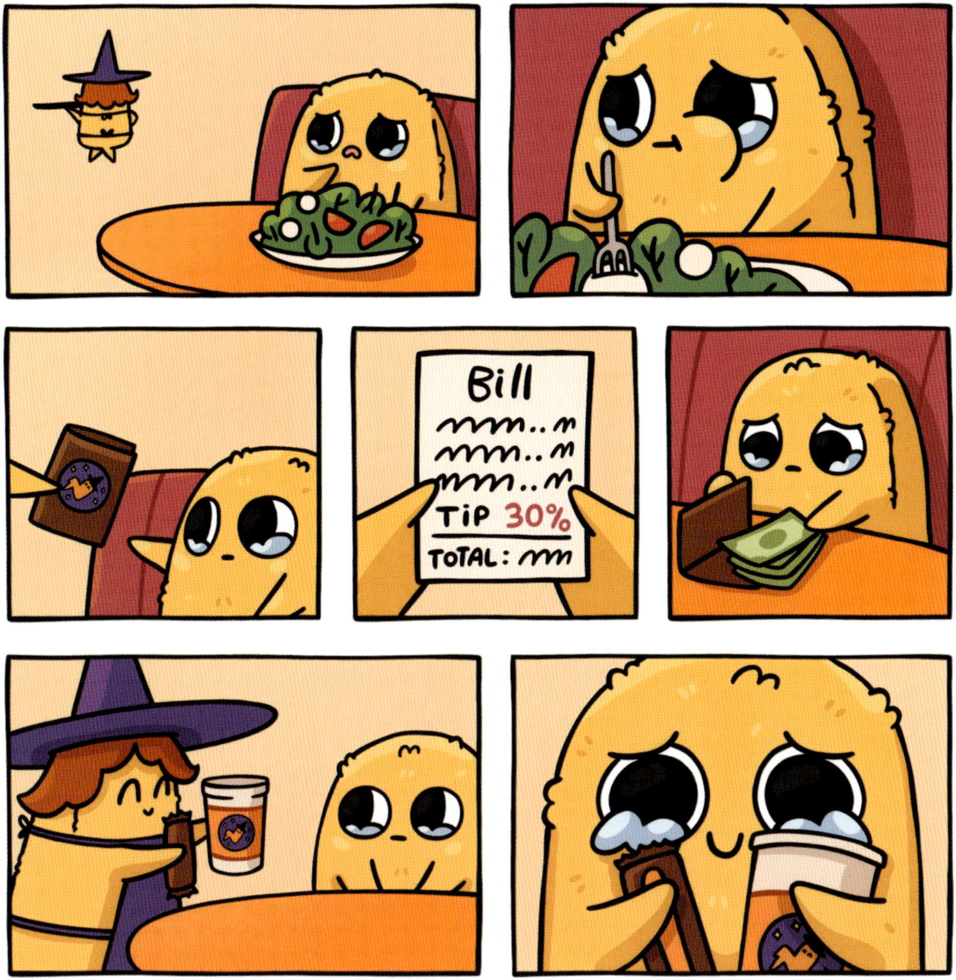
Bill
TIP 30%
TOTAL:

THERAPY SESSION 3

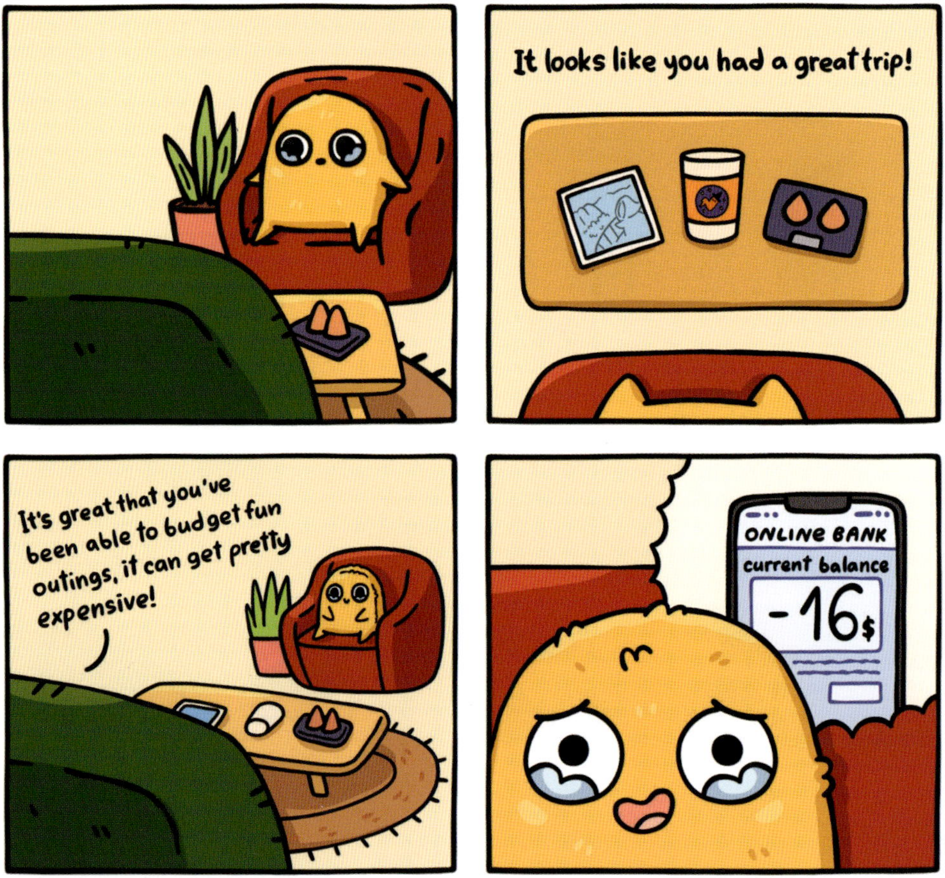

It looks like you had a great trip!
It's great that you've been able to budget fun outings, it can get pretty expensive!
ONLINE BANK
current balance
-16$

CHAPTER 4
DRESSED FOR SUCCESS

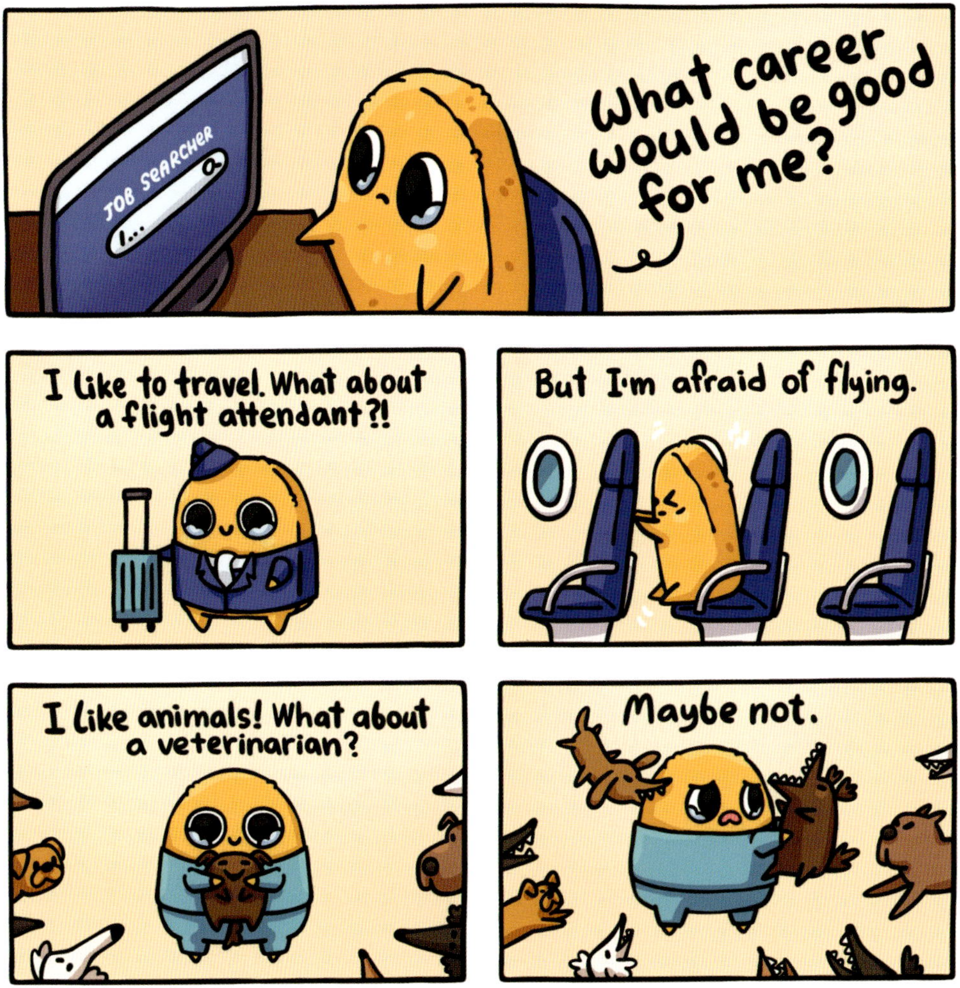
JOB SEARCHER
I...
What career would be good for me?
I like to travel. What about a flight attendant?!
But I'm afraid of flying.
I like animals! What about a veterinarian?
Maybe not.

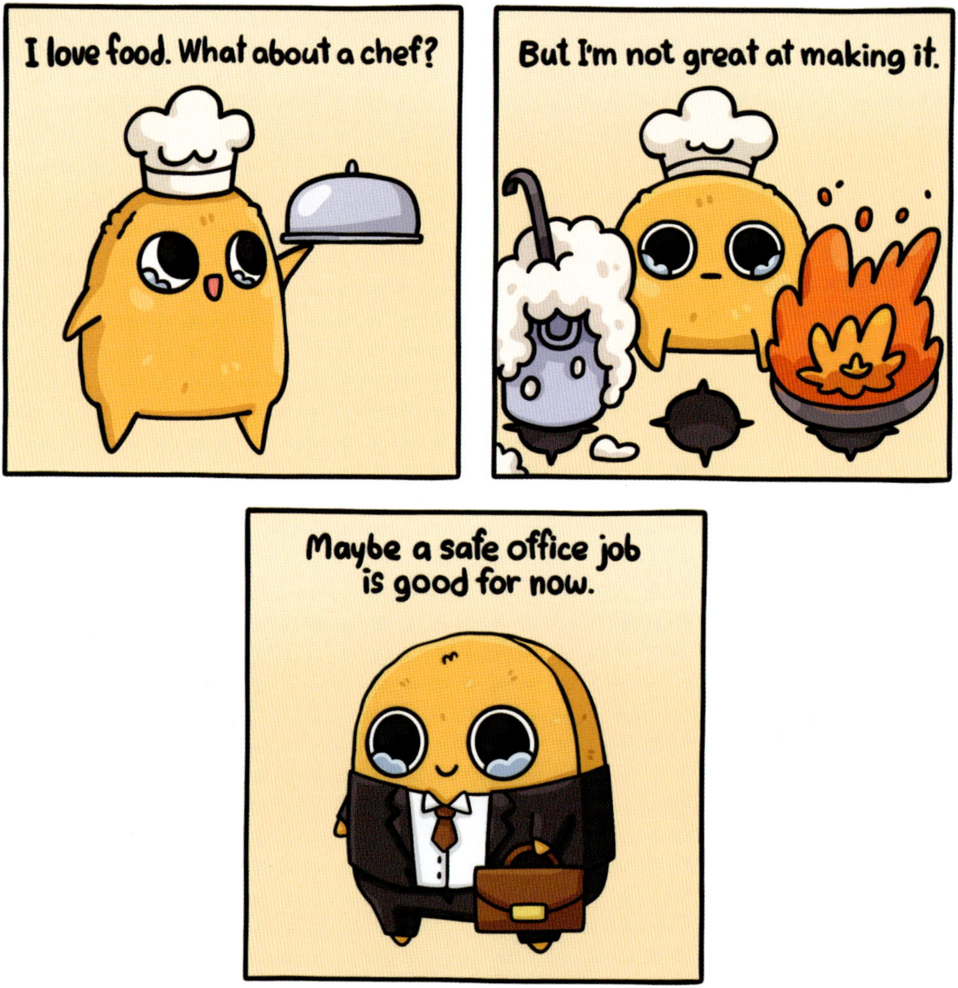
I love food. What about a chef?
But I'm not great at making it.
Maybe a safe office job
is good for now.

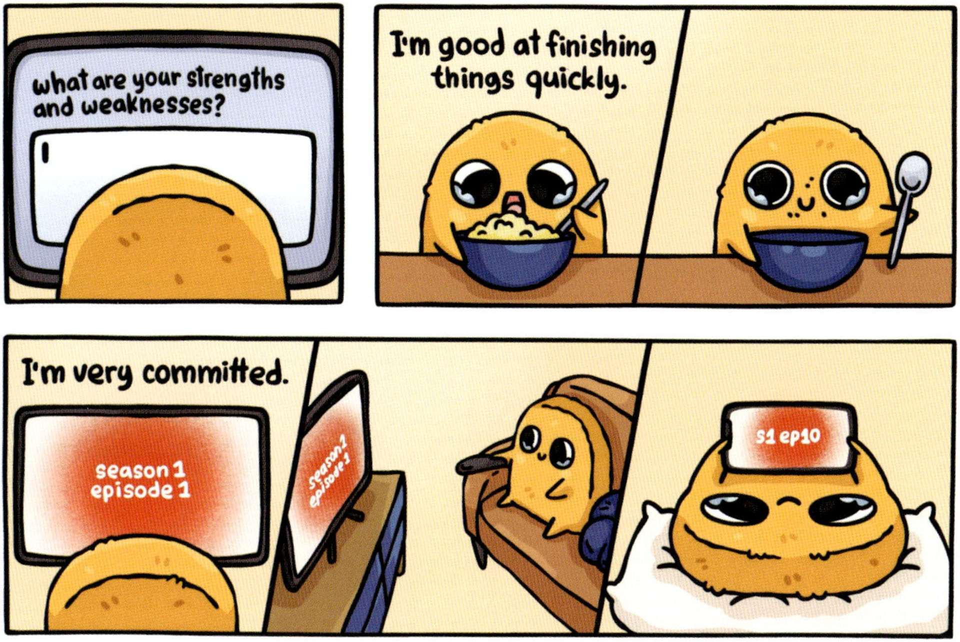

what are your strengths and weaknesses?
I'm good at finishing things quickly.
I'm very committed.
season 1 episode 1
season 1 episode 1
S1 ep10

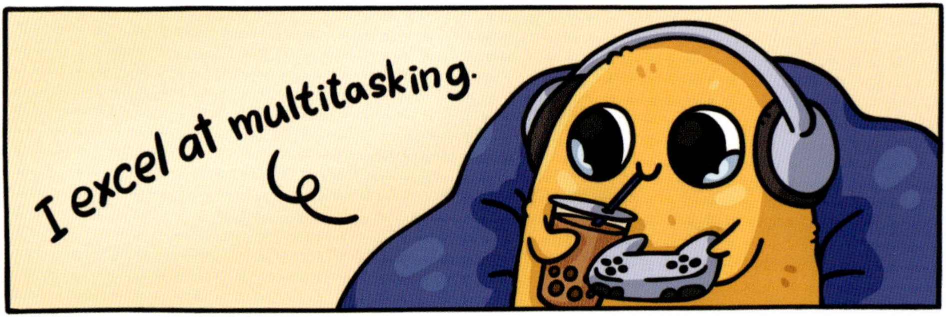
I excel at multitasking.

CHICKEN NUGGET AFFIRMATIONS TO GET YOU THROUGH YOUR WORK WEEK

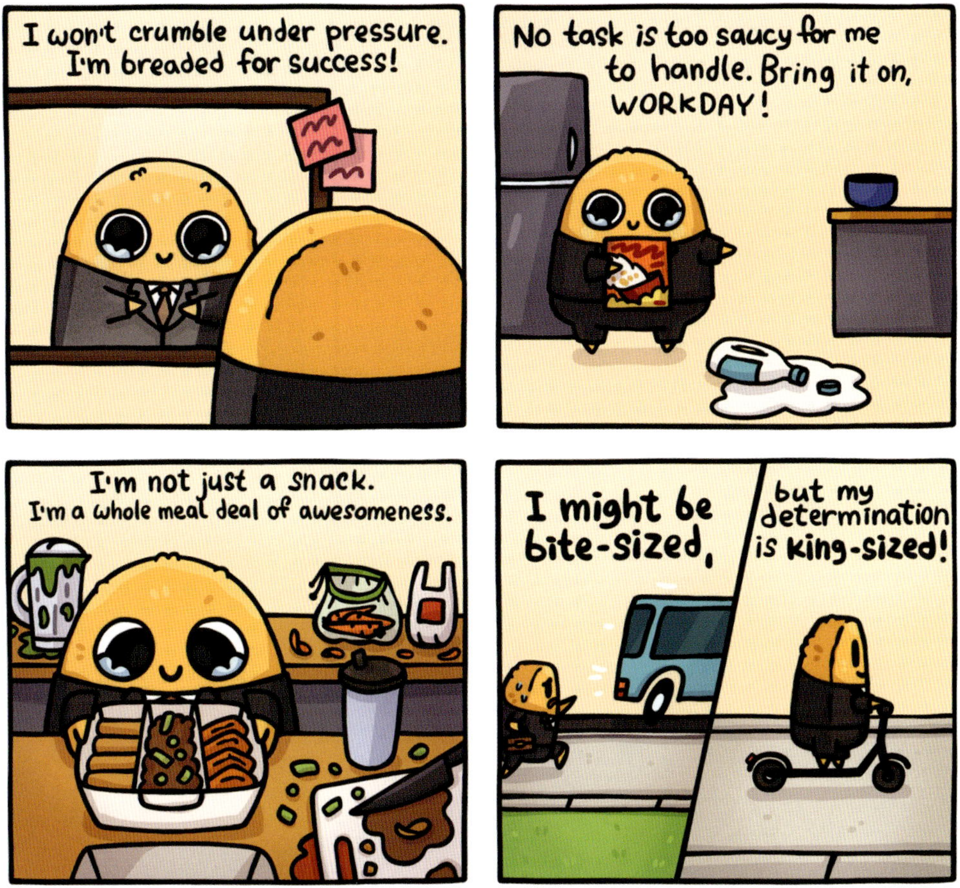
I won't crumble under pressure. I'm breaded for success!
No task is too saucy for me to handle. Bring it on, WORKDAY!
I'm not just a snack. I'm a whole meal deal of awesomeness.
I might be bite-sized,
but my determination is king-sized!

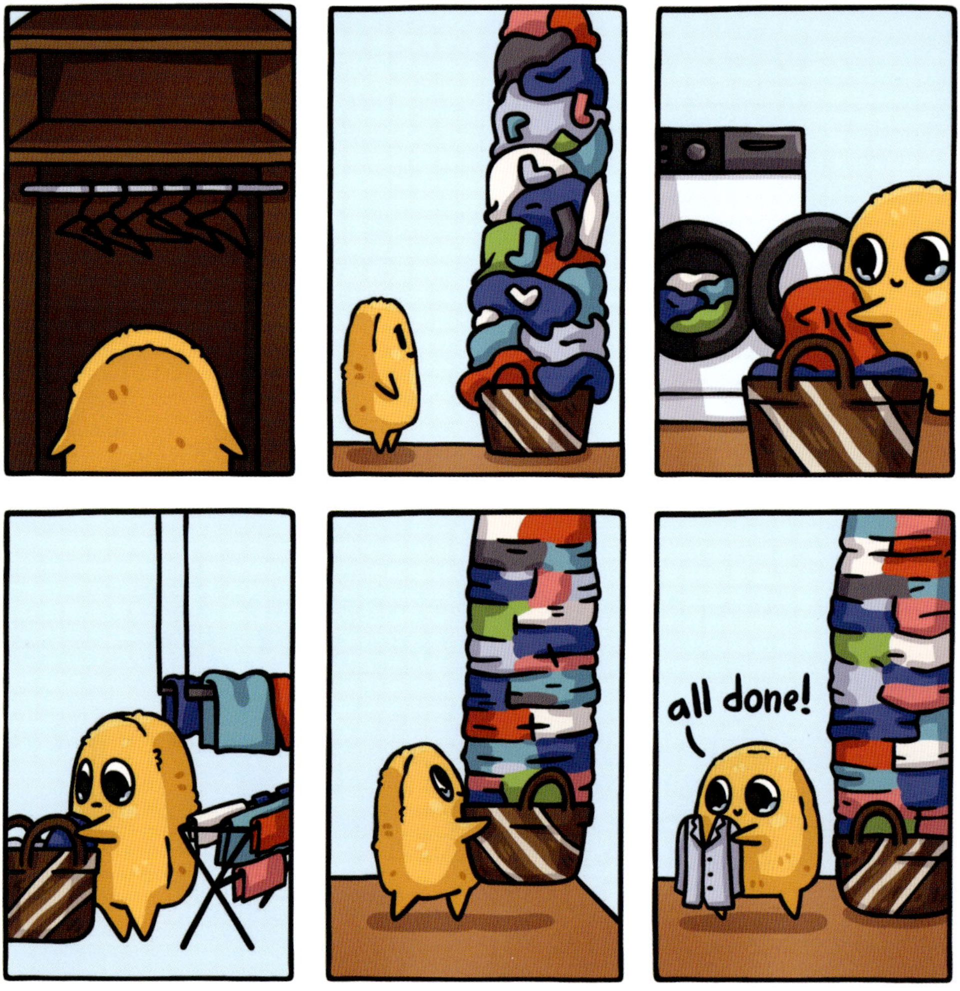
all done!

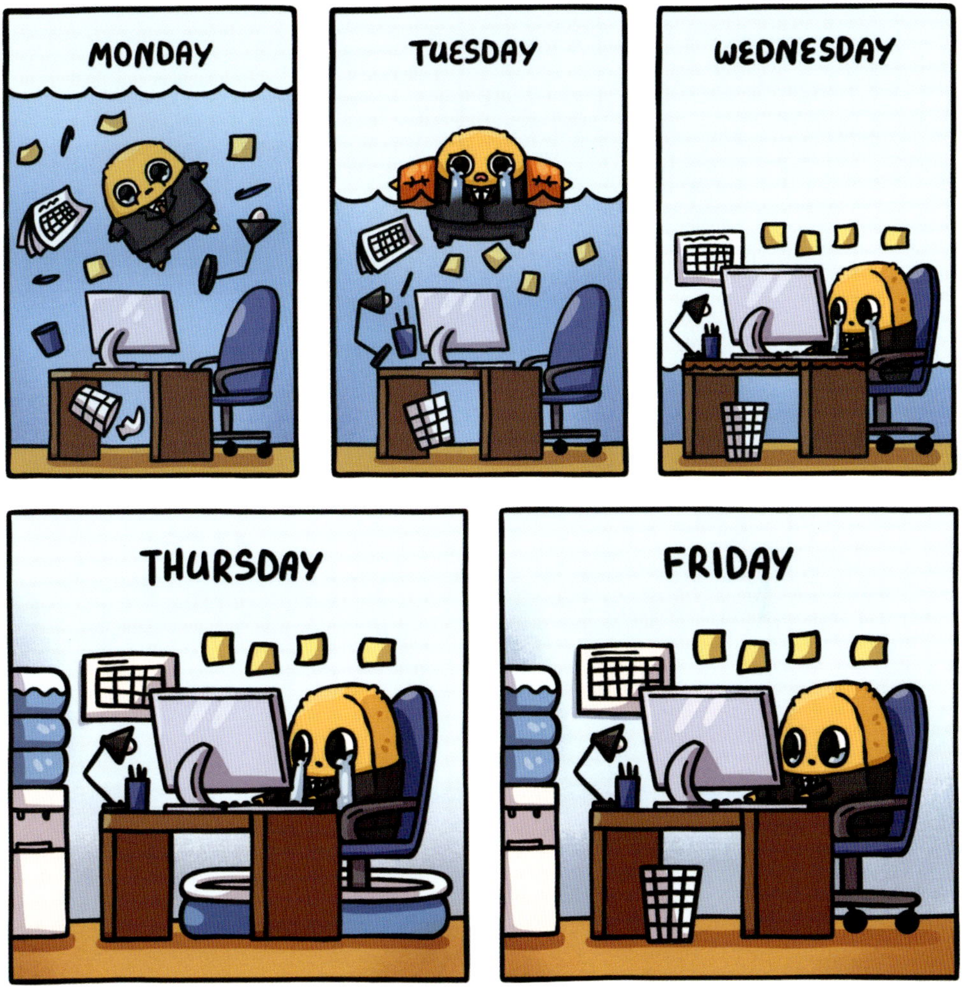
MONDAY
TUESDAY
WEDNESDAY
THURSDAY
FRIDAY

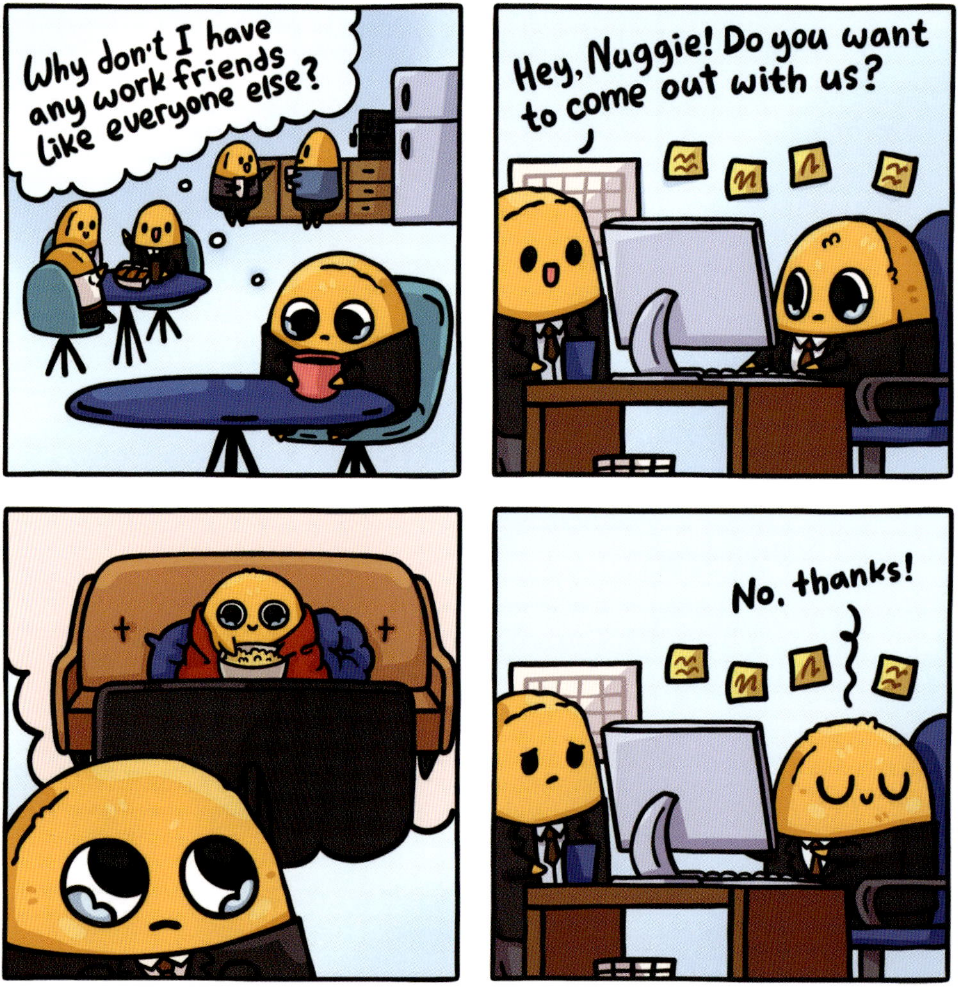
Why don't I have any work friends like everyone else?
Hey, Nuggie! Do you want to come out with us?
No, thanks!

CLIENT (mmm)

FROM: Sad nuggie
TO: CLIENT

HI, CLIENT.
CAN YOU LEARN HOW
TO READ?!

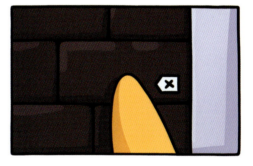

FROM: Sad nuggie
TO: CLIENT

GOOD MORNING, CLIENT!
AS PER MY LAST EMAIL...

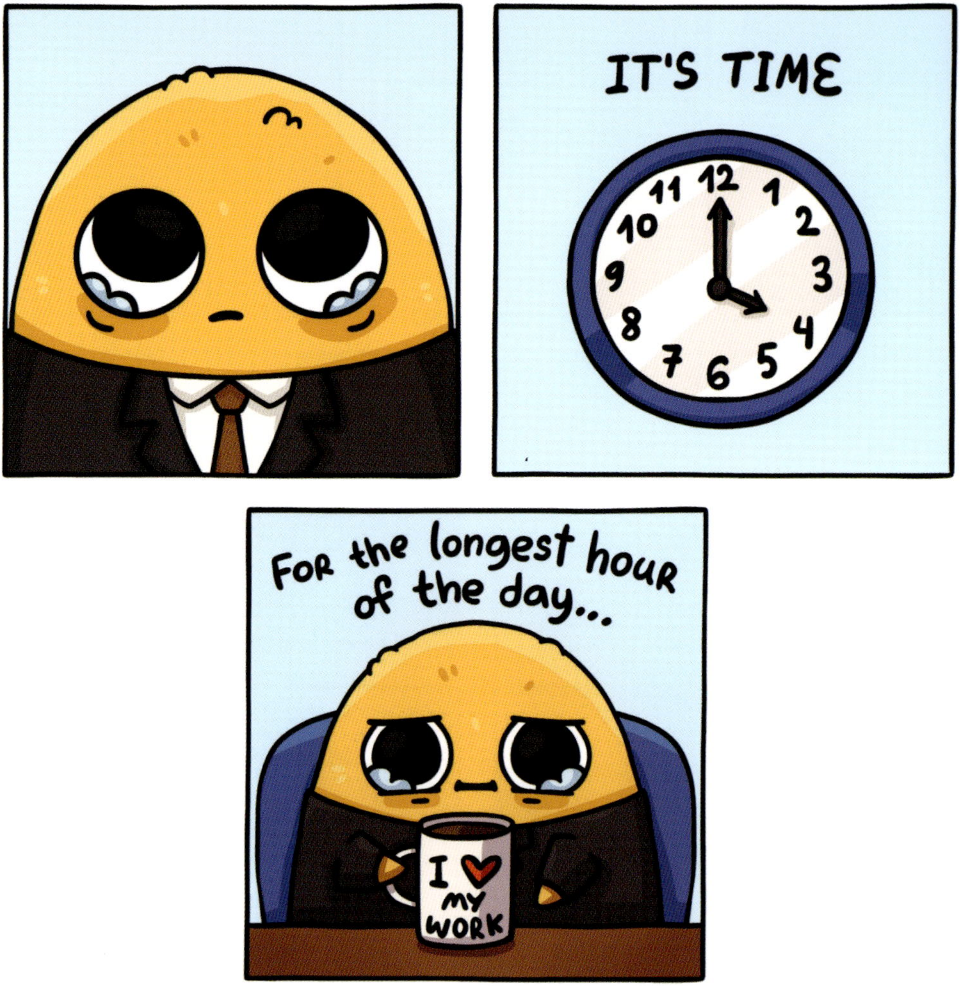
IT'S TIME
For the longest hour of the day...
I ♥ MY WORK

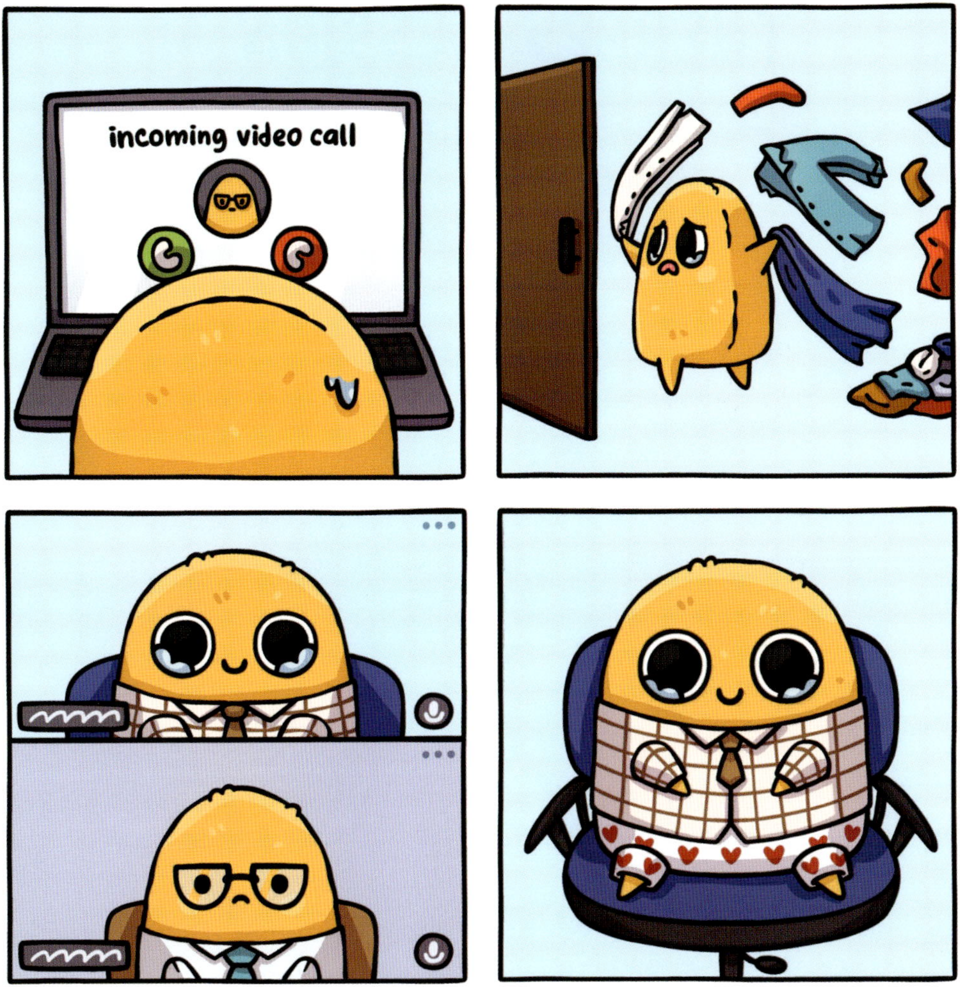
incoming video call

THERAPY SESSION 4

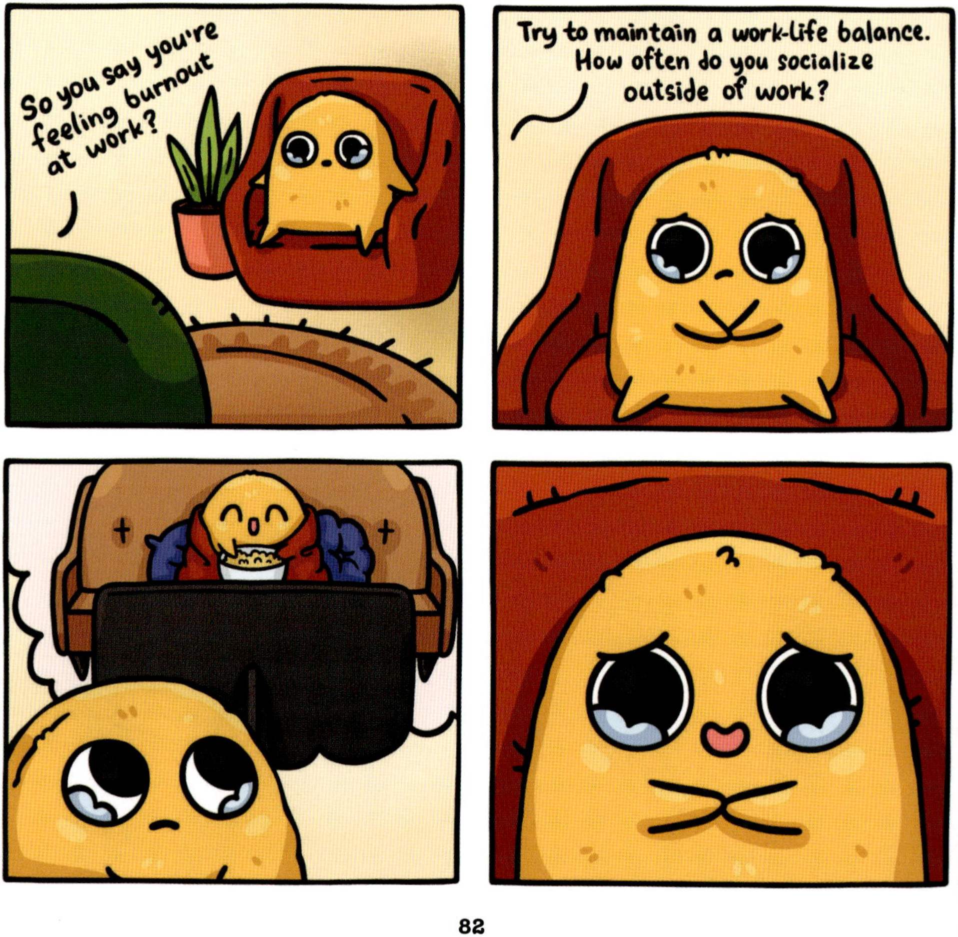
So you say you're feeling burnout at work?
Try to maintain a work-life balance. How often do you socialize outside of work?

CHAPTER 5
WEEKEND VIBES

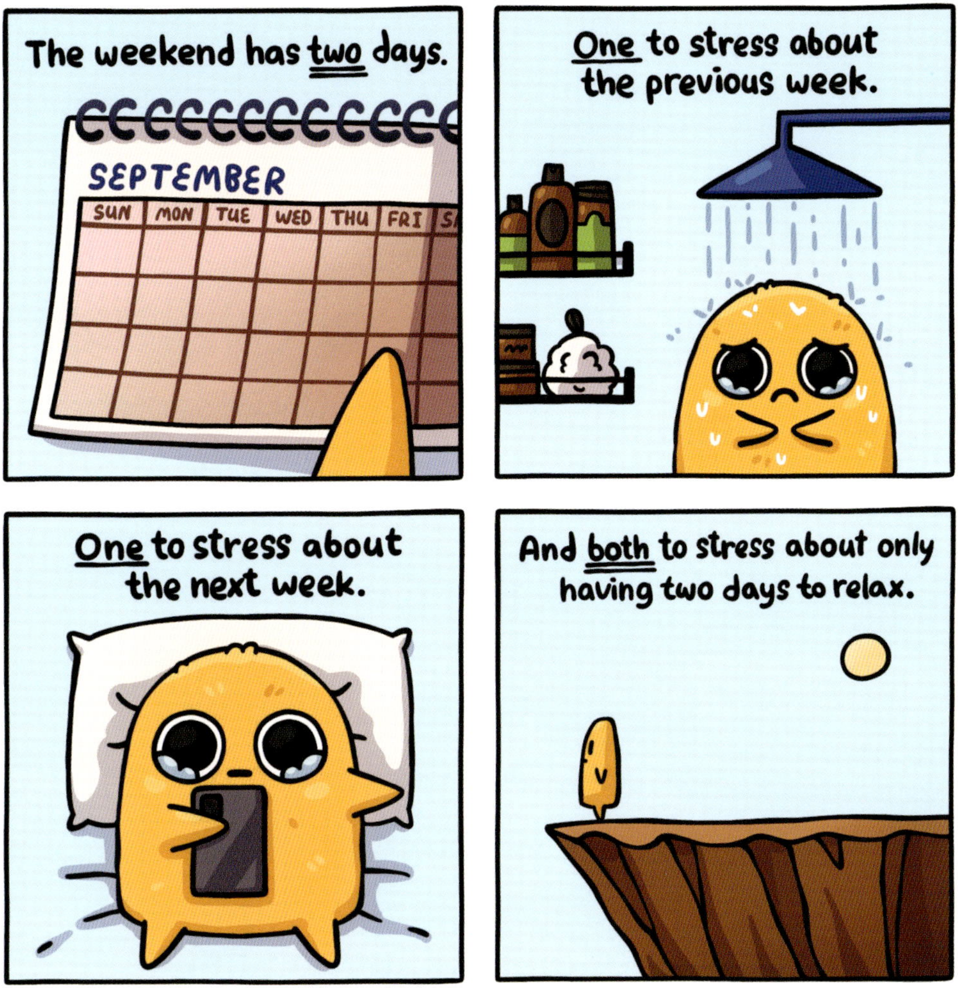
The weekend has two days.
SEPTEMBER
SUN MON TUE WED THU FRI
One to stress about the previous week.
One to stress about the next week.
And both to stress about only having two days to relax.

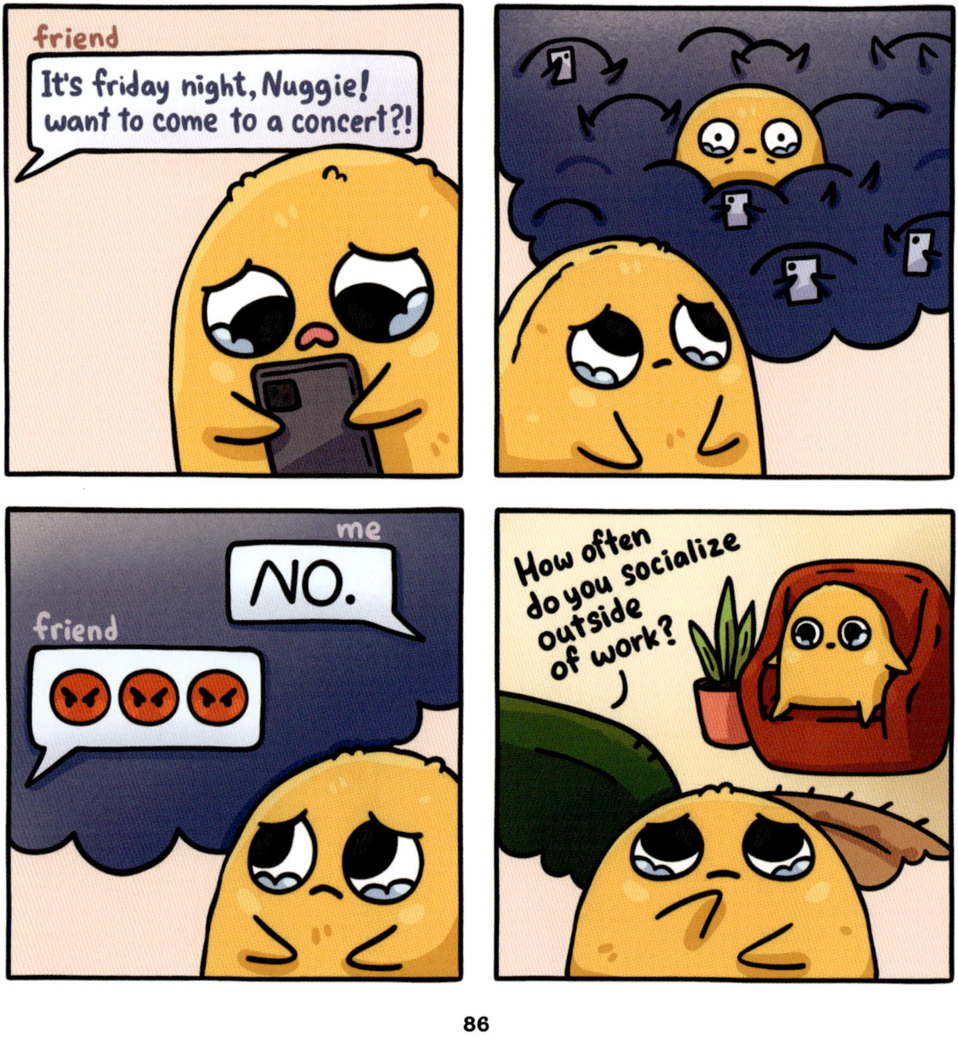
friend
It's friday night, Nuggie! want to come to a concert?!
me
NO.
friend
How often do you socialize outside of work?

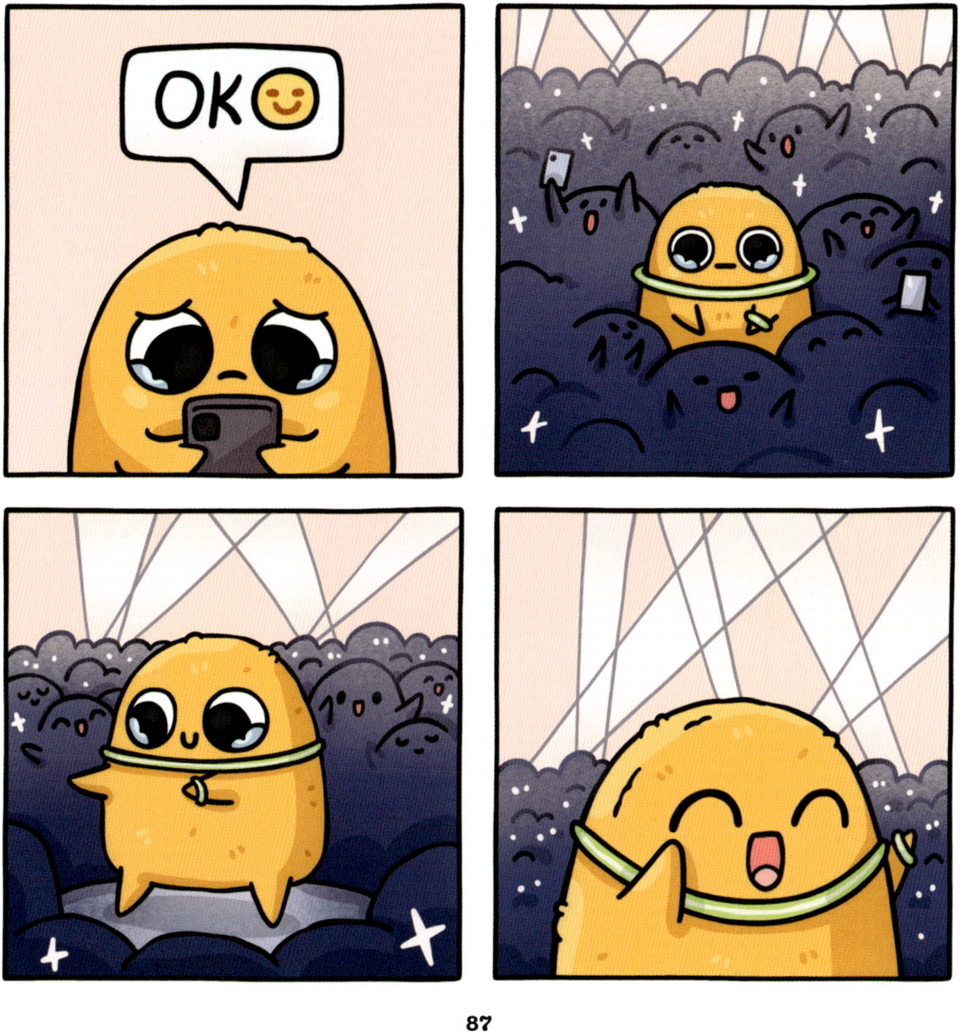
OK

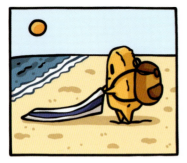

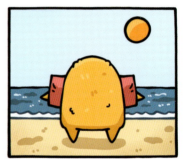

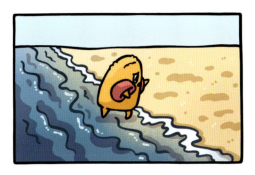

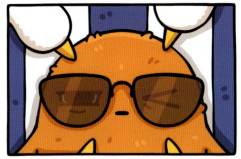

Oops, looks like I got a little too crispy. That's enough beach for today.

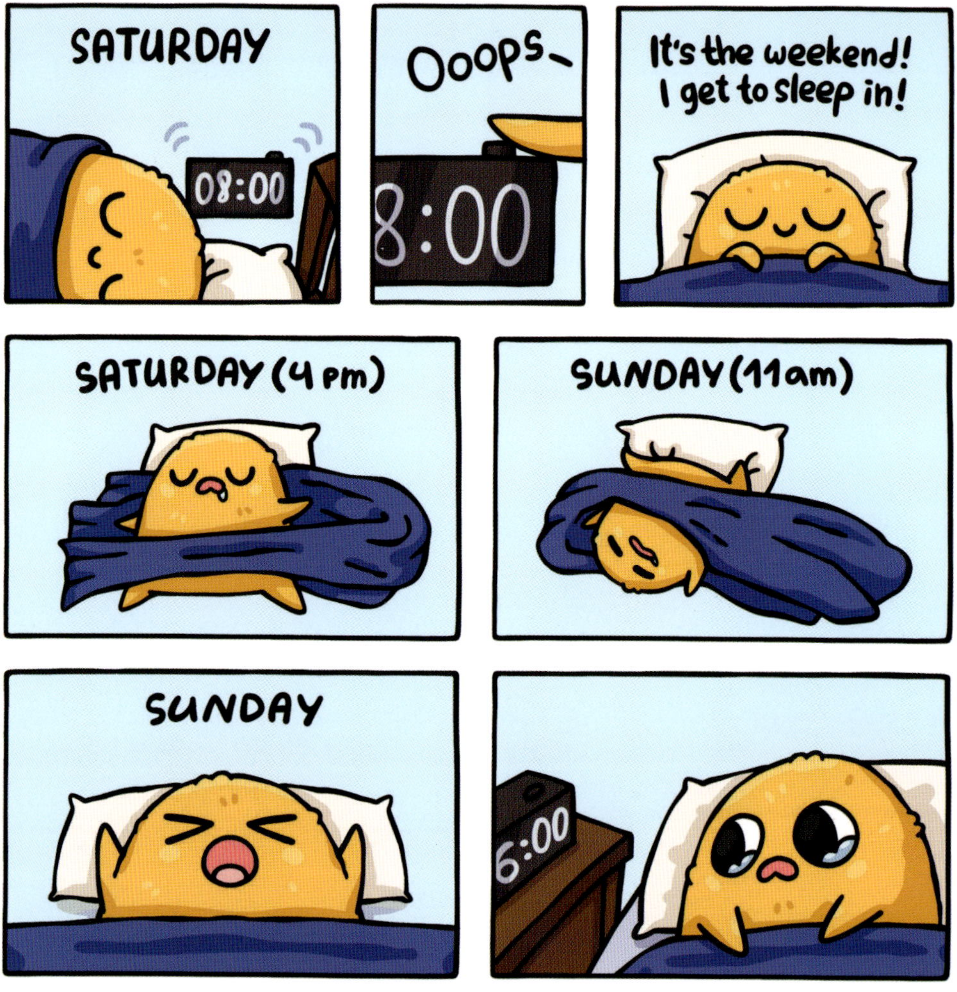
SATURDAY
08:00
Ooops~
8:00
It's the weekend! I get to sleep in!
SATURDAY (4 pm)
SUNDAY (11am)
SUNDAY
6:00

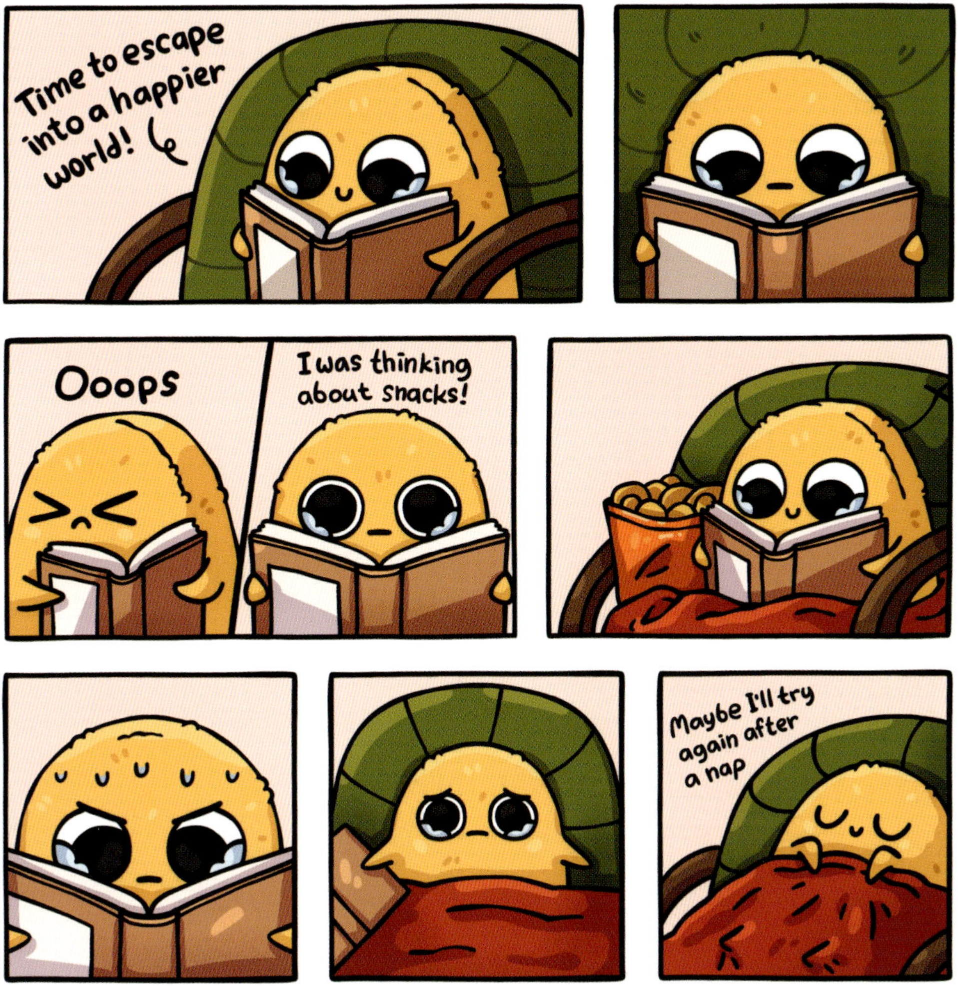
Time to escape into a happier world!
Ooops
I was thinking about snacks!
Maybe I'll try again after a nap

NUGGIE'S GUIDE TO A PRODUCTIVE WEEK

1. Tidy up your room.

2. Catch up on laundry.

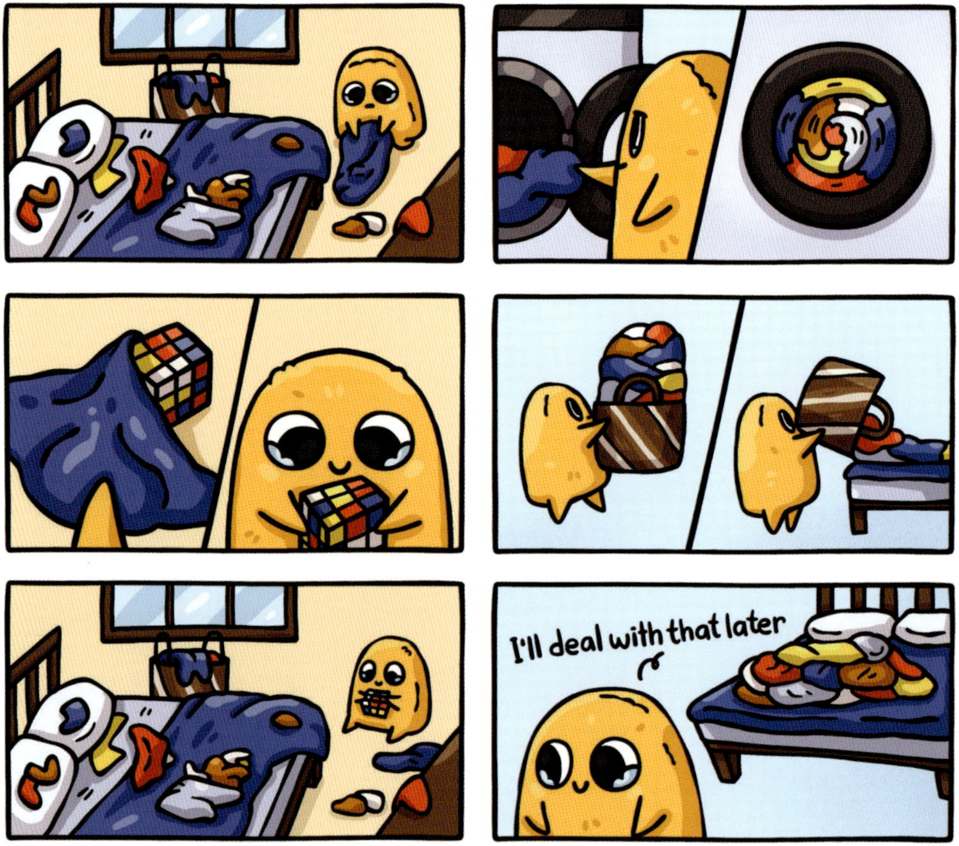
I'll deal with that later

3. Pick up healthy groceries for the week.

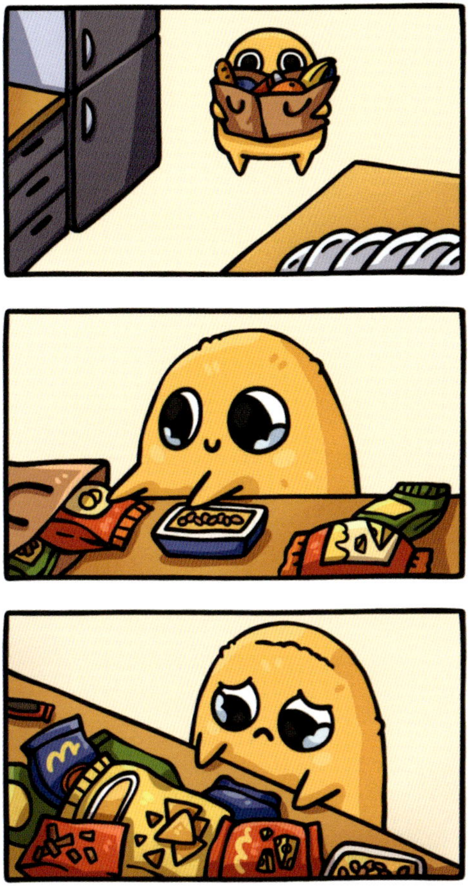

4. Meal prep for the next week!

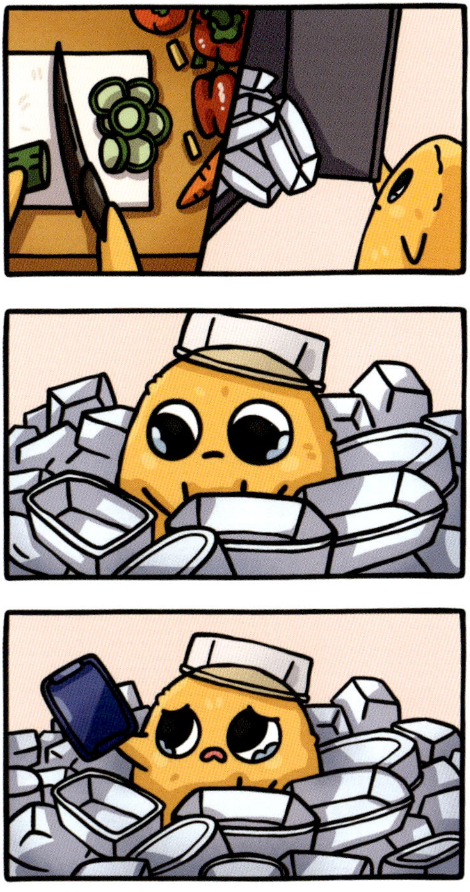

5.Catch up on rest.

1:00AM
6:00AM

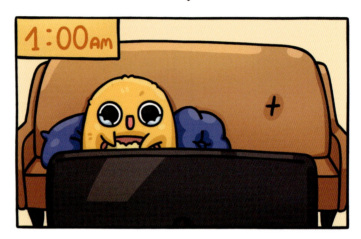

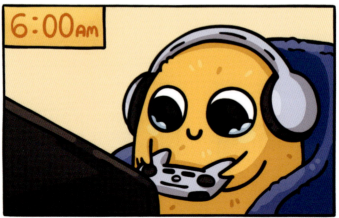

Time to make my yard beautiful!

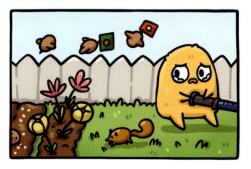

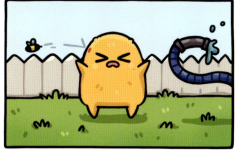

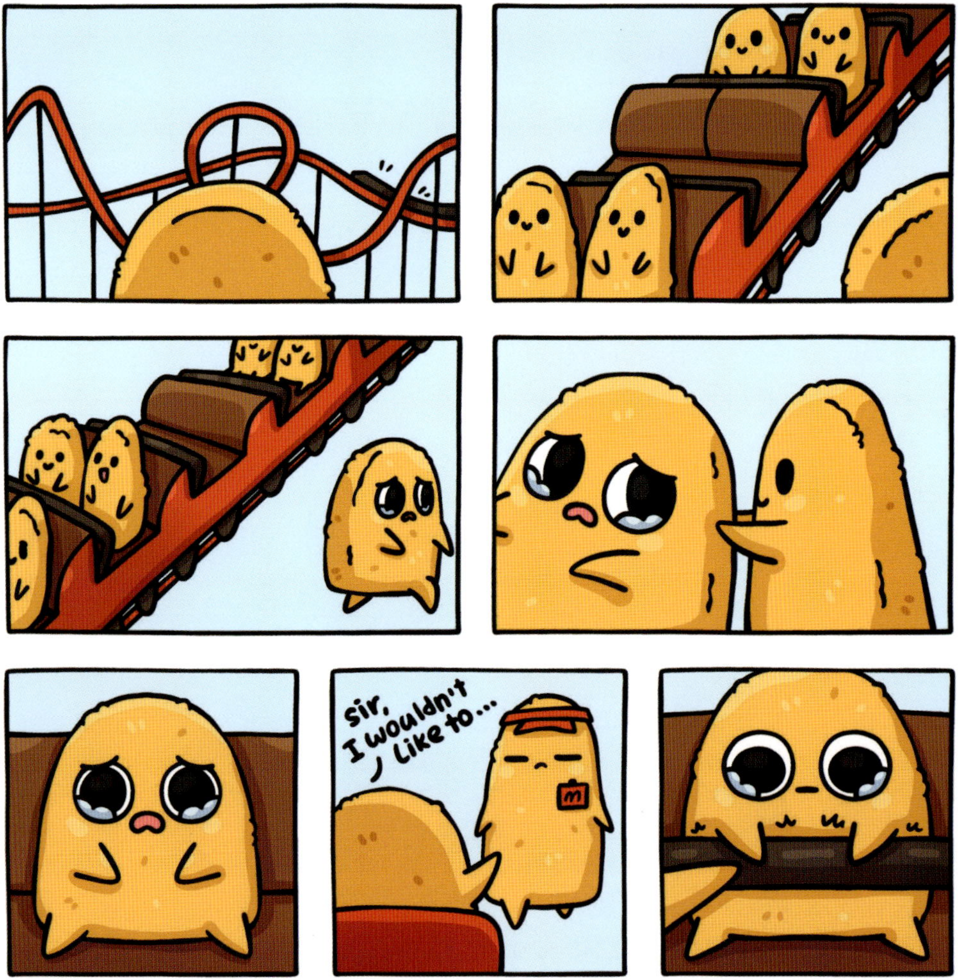
sir, I wouldn't like to...

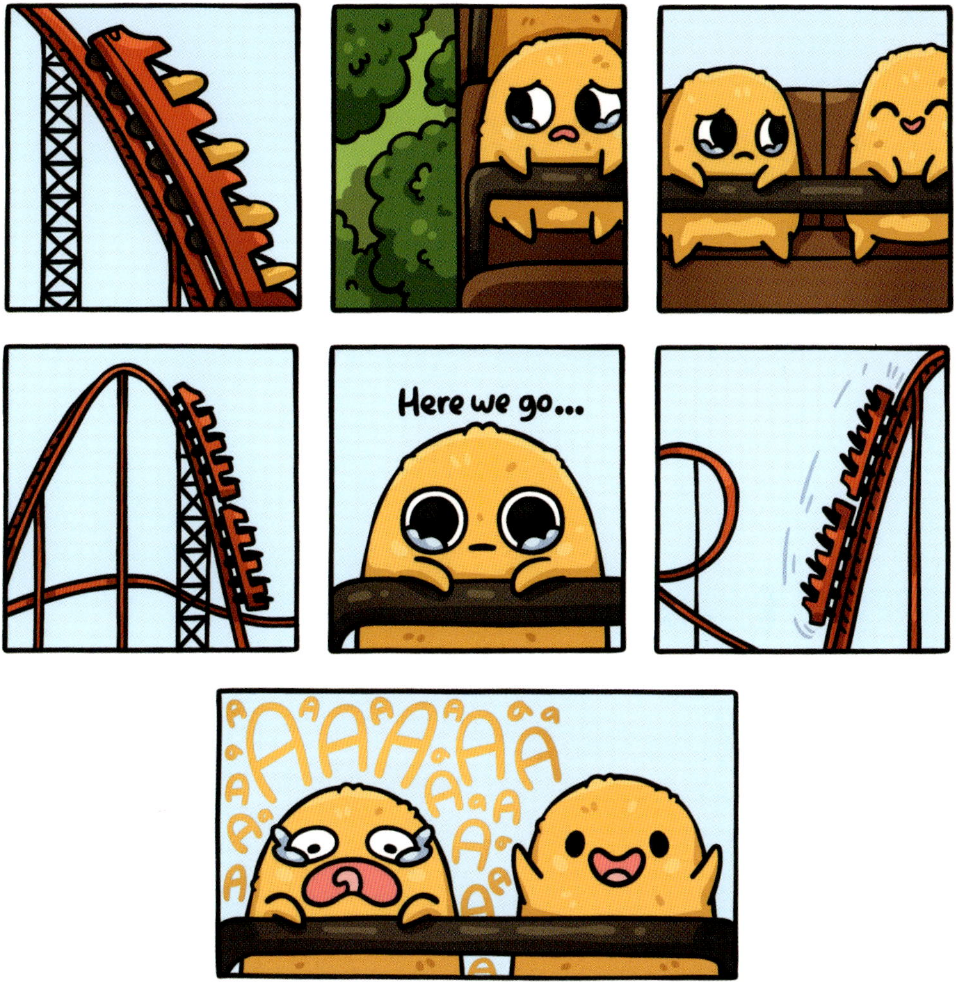
Here we go...

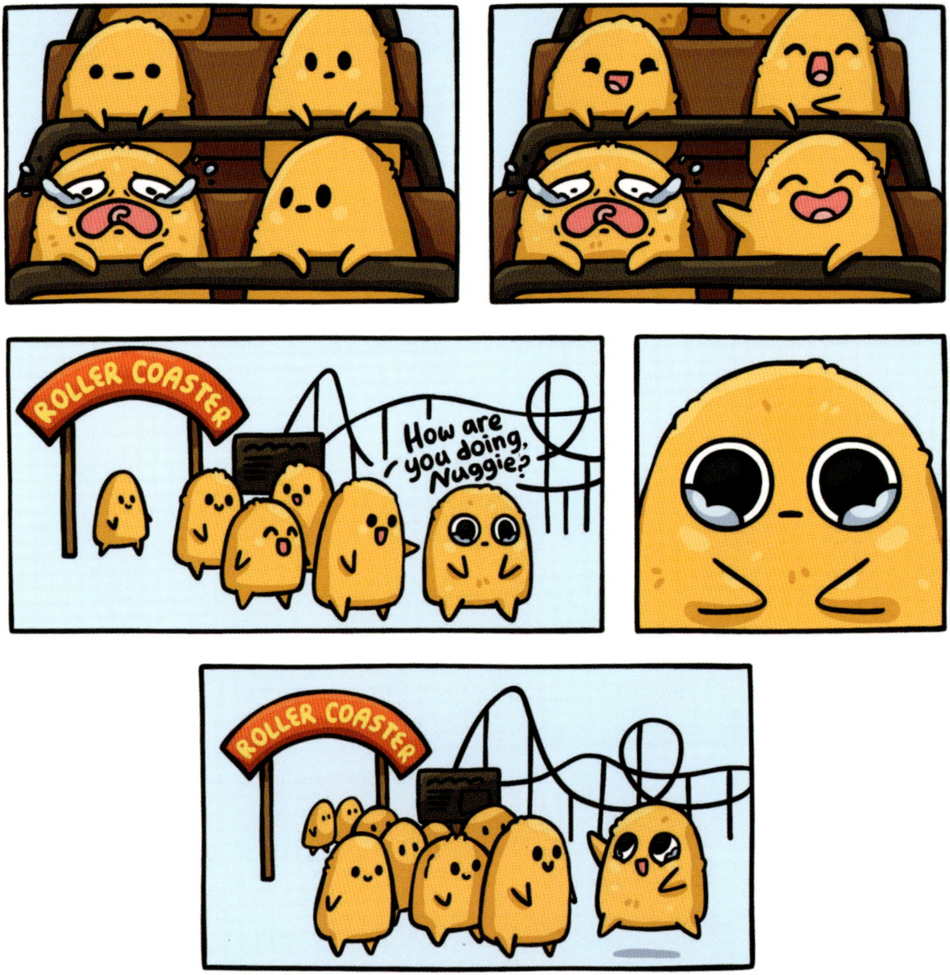
ROLLER COASTER
How are you doing, Nuggie?
ROLLER COASTER

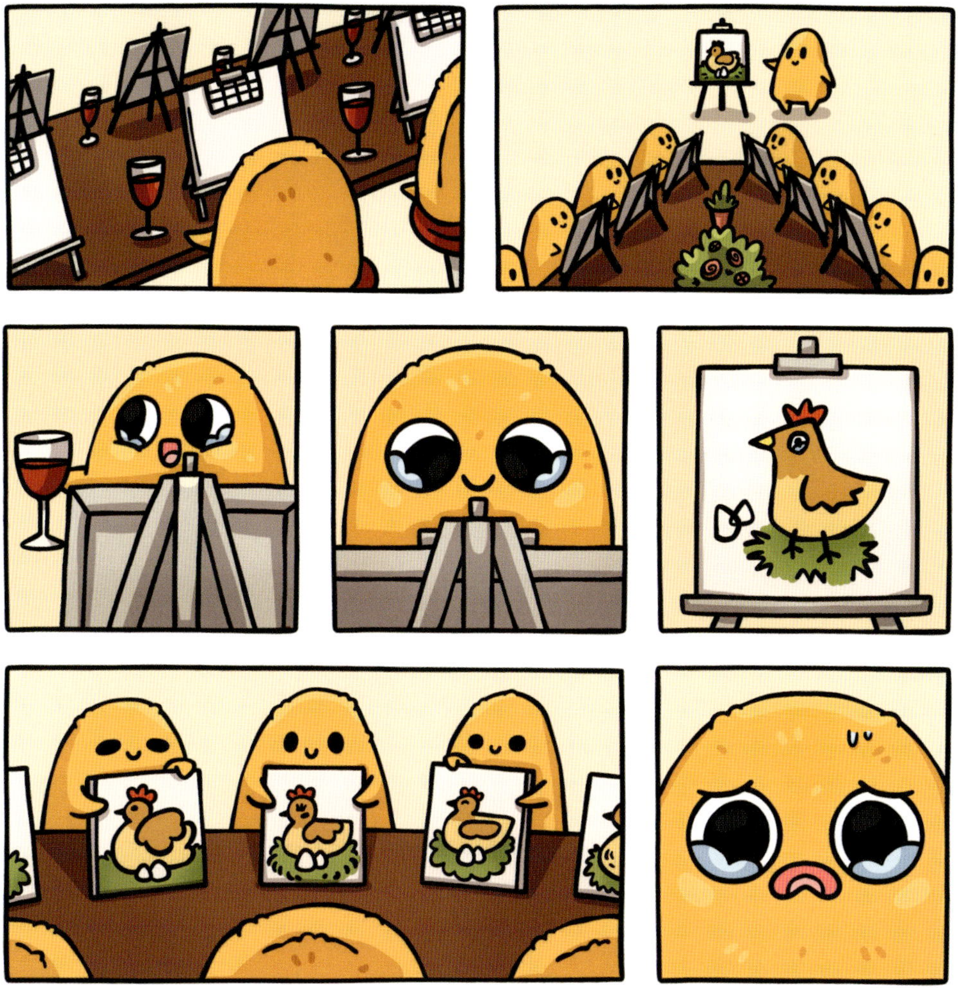

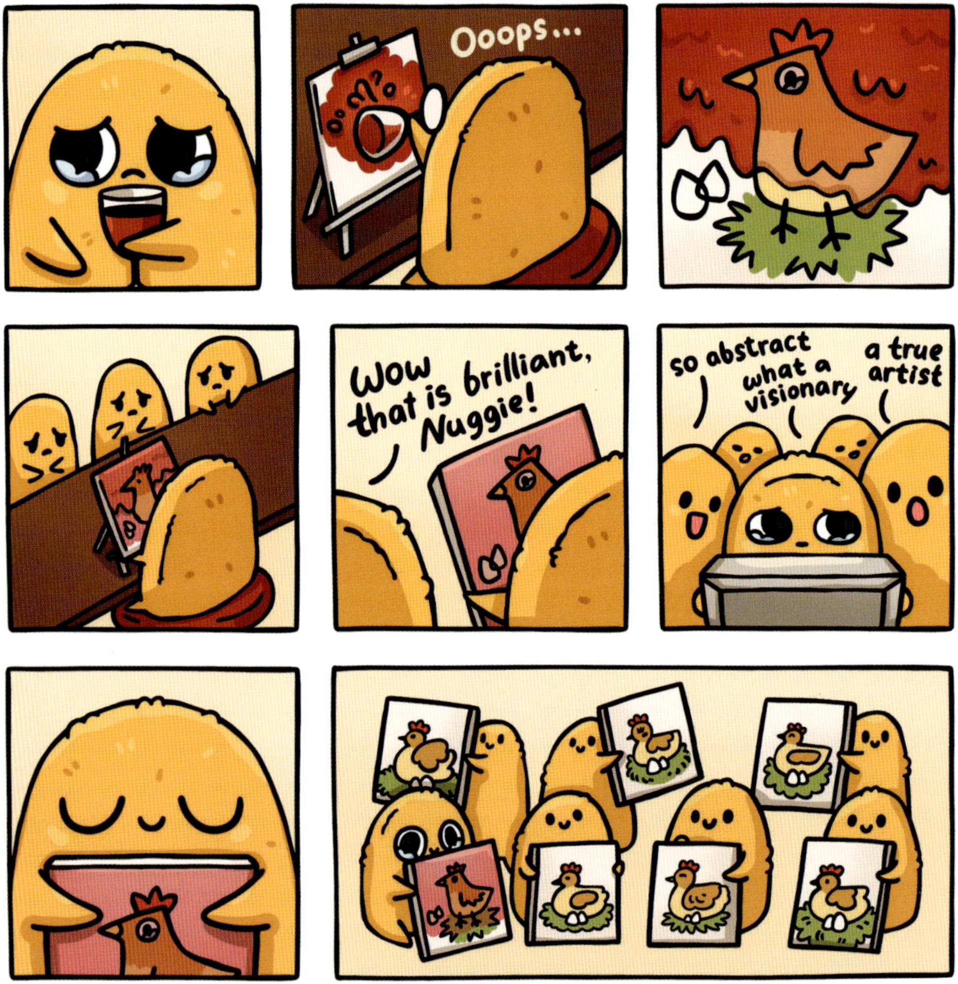
Ooops...
Wow that is brilliant, Nuggie!
so abstract
what a visionary
a true artist

THERAPY SESSION 5

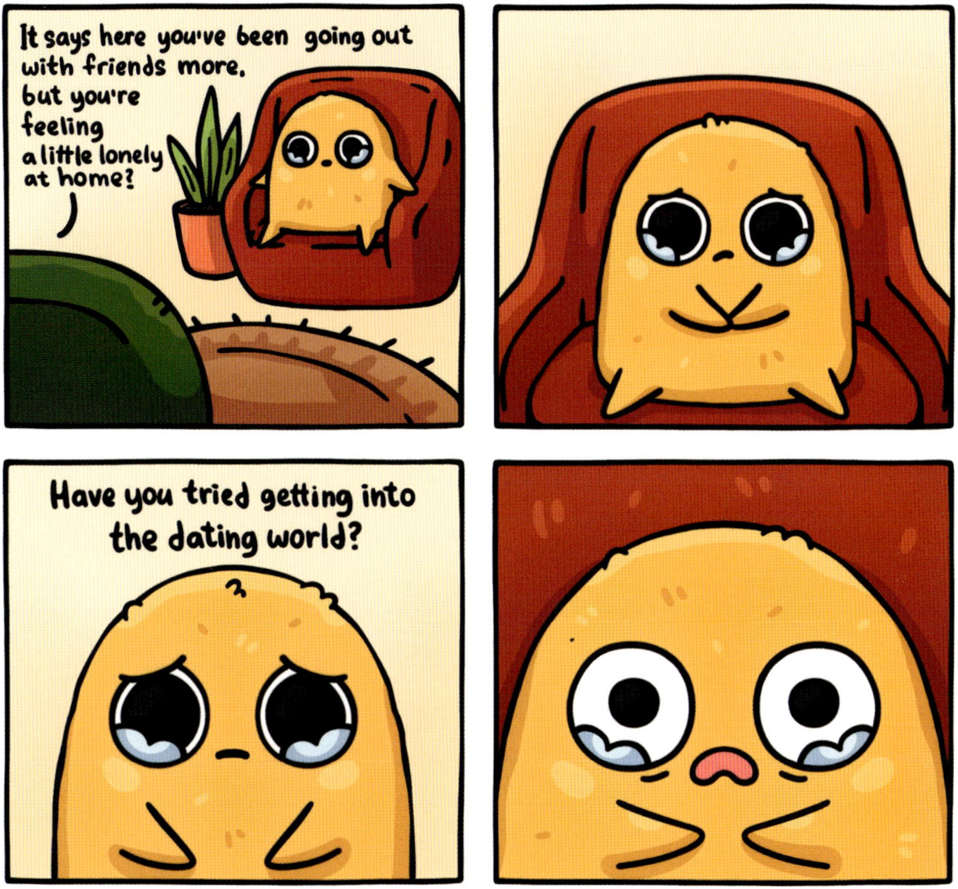
It says here you've been going out with friends more, but you're feeling a little lonely at home?
Have you tried getting into the dating world?

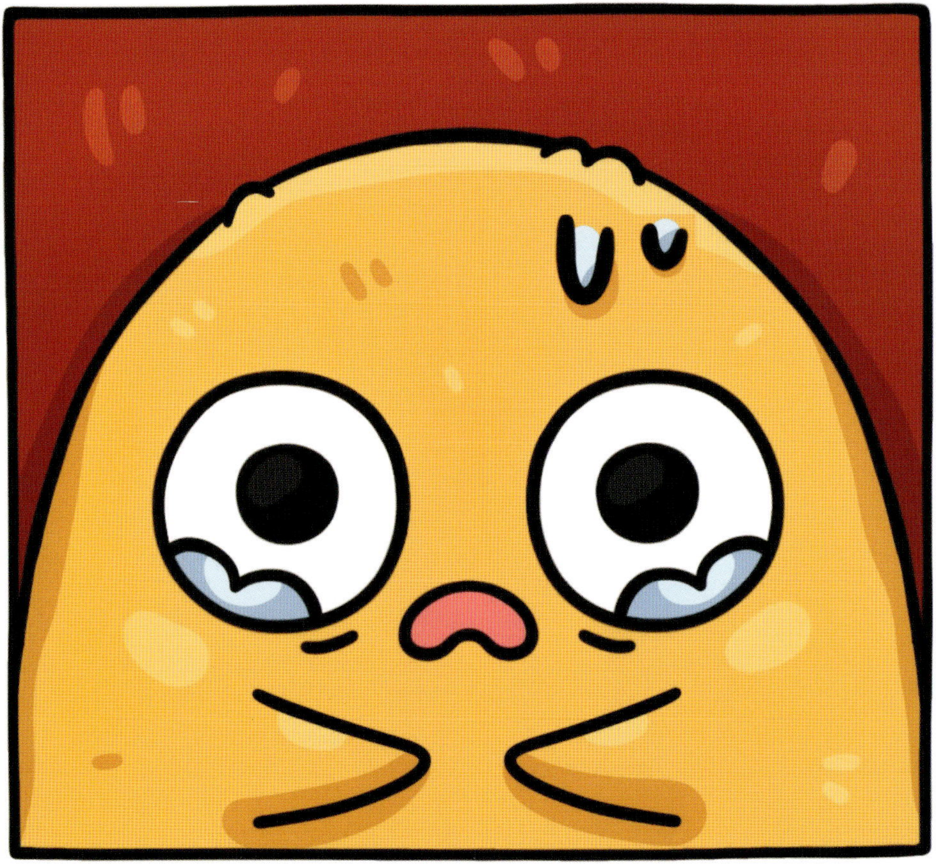

CHAPTER 6
TWO NUGGIES IN A BOX

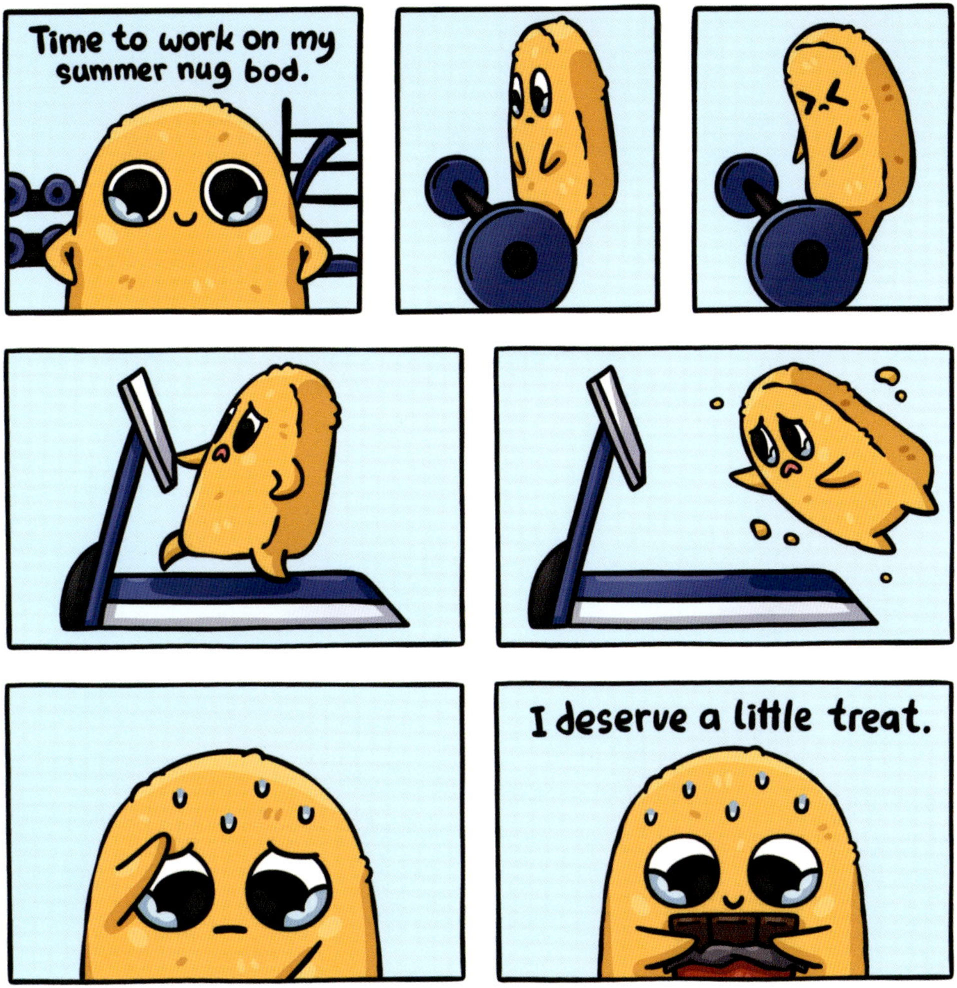
Time to work on my summer nug bod.
I deserve a little treat.

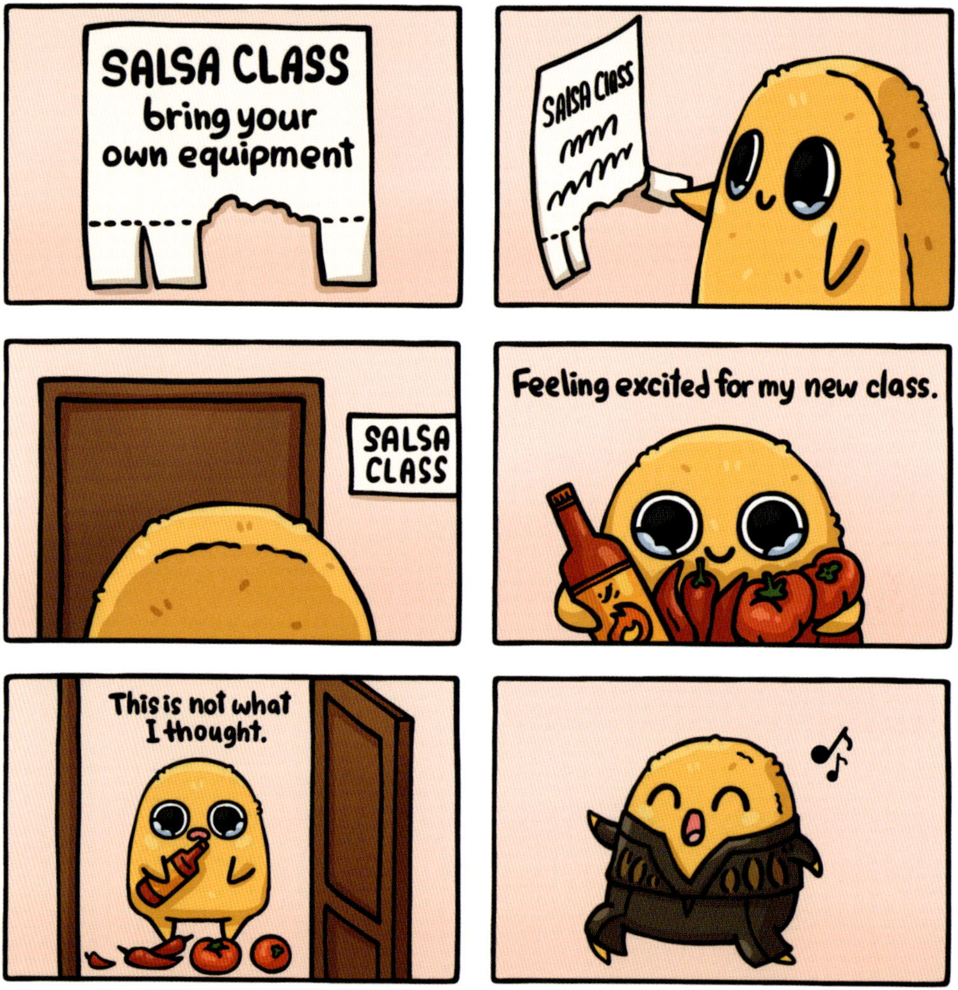
SALSA CLASS
bring your
own equipment
SALSA CLASS
SALSA
CLASS
Feeling excited for my new class.
This is not what
I thought.

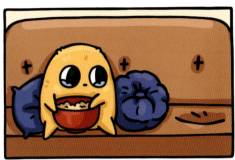

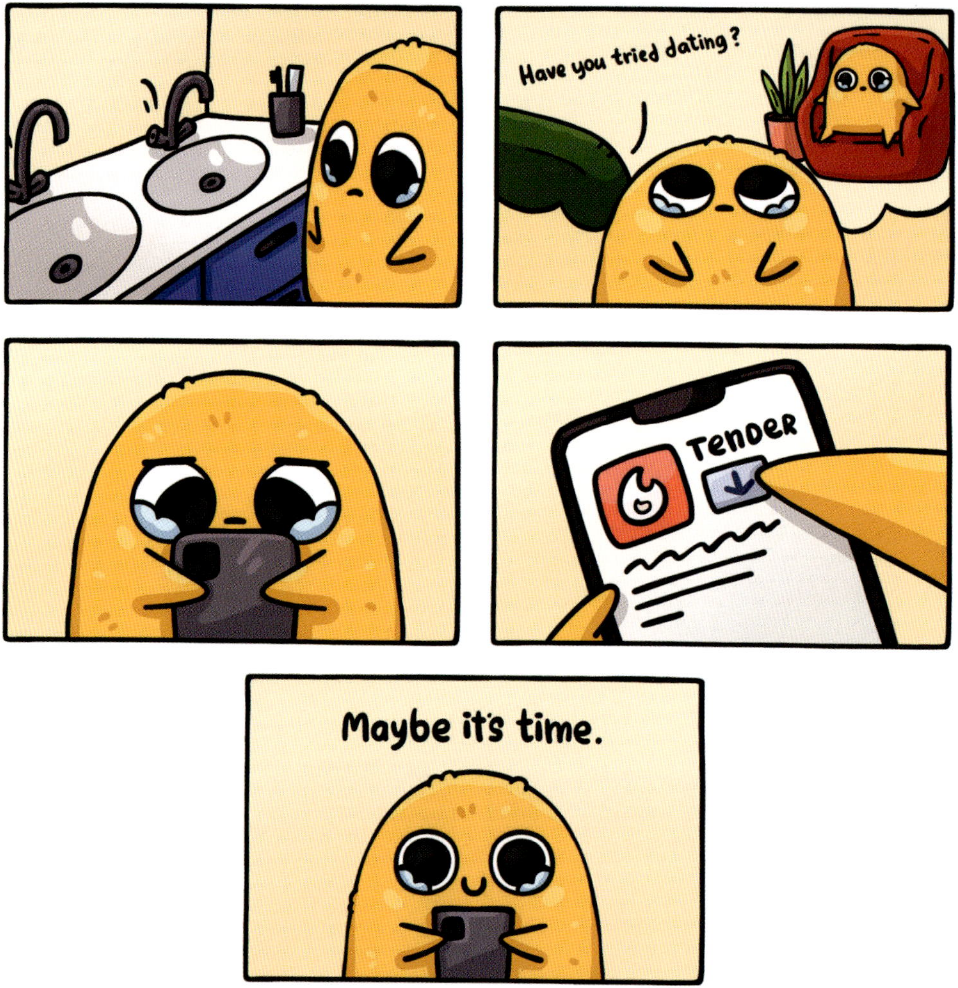
Have you tried dating?
TENDER
Maybe it's time.

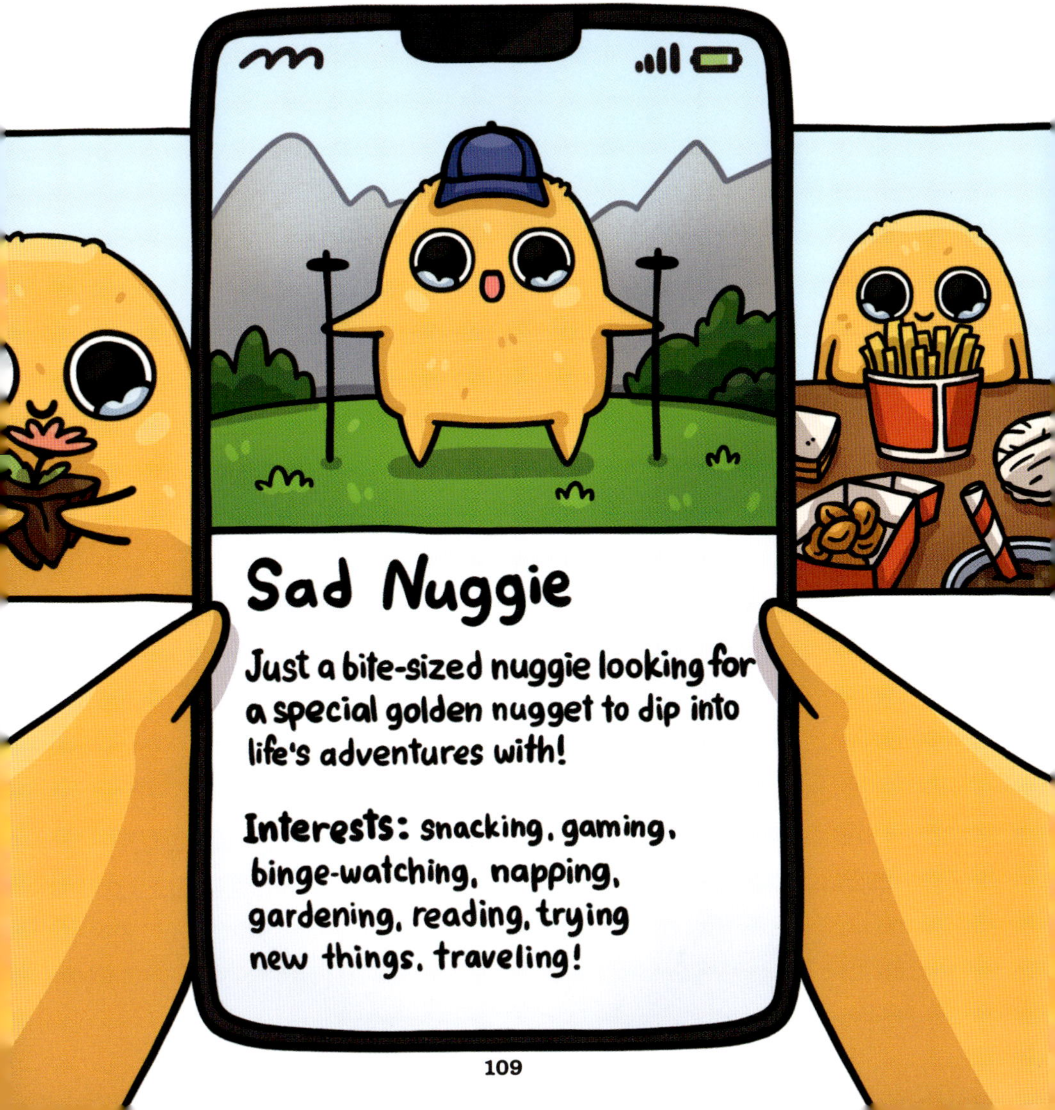
Sad Nuggie
Just a bite-sized nuggie looking for a special golden nugget to dip into life's adventures with!
Interests: snacking, gaming, binge-watching, napping, gardening, reading, trying new things, traveling!

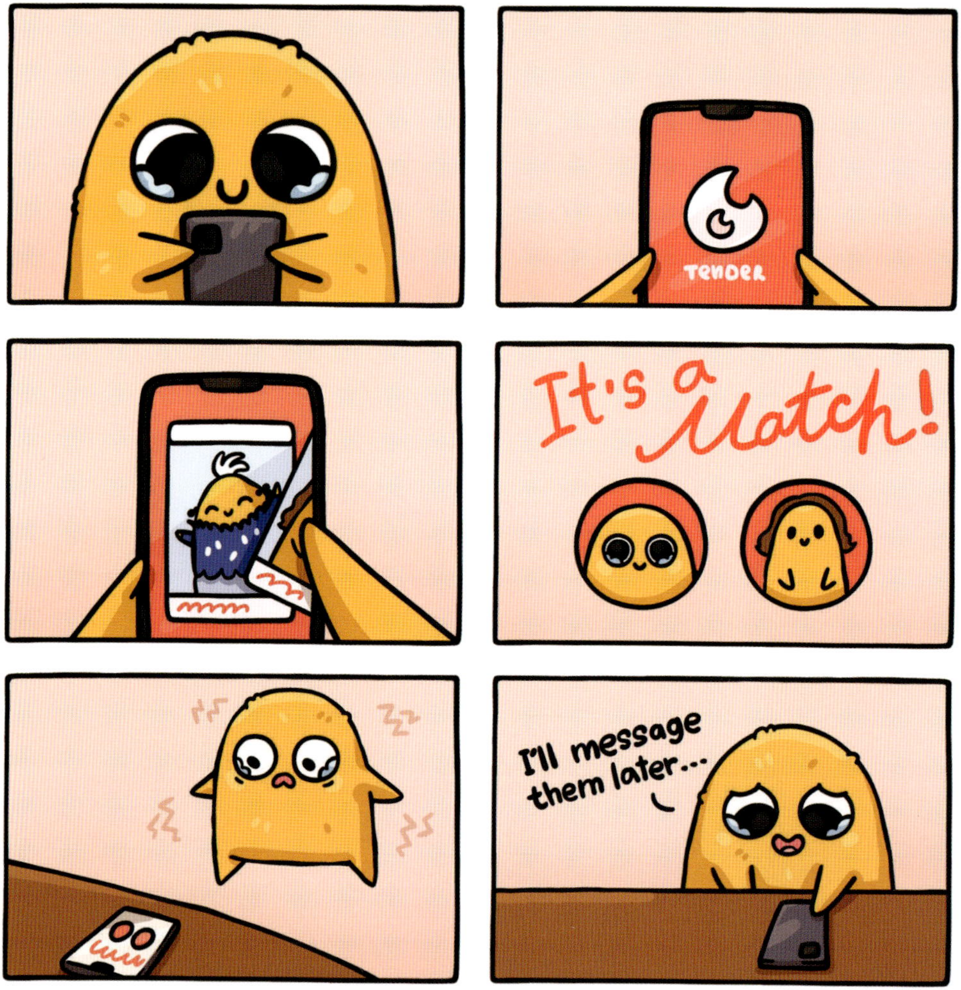
TENDER
It's a Match!
I'll message them later...

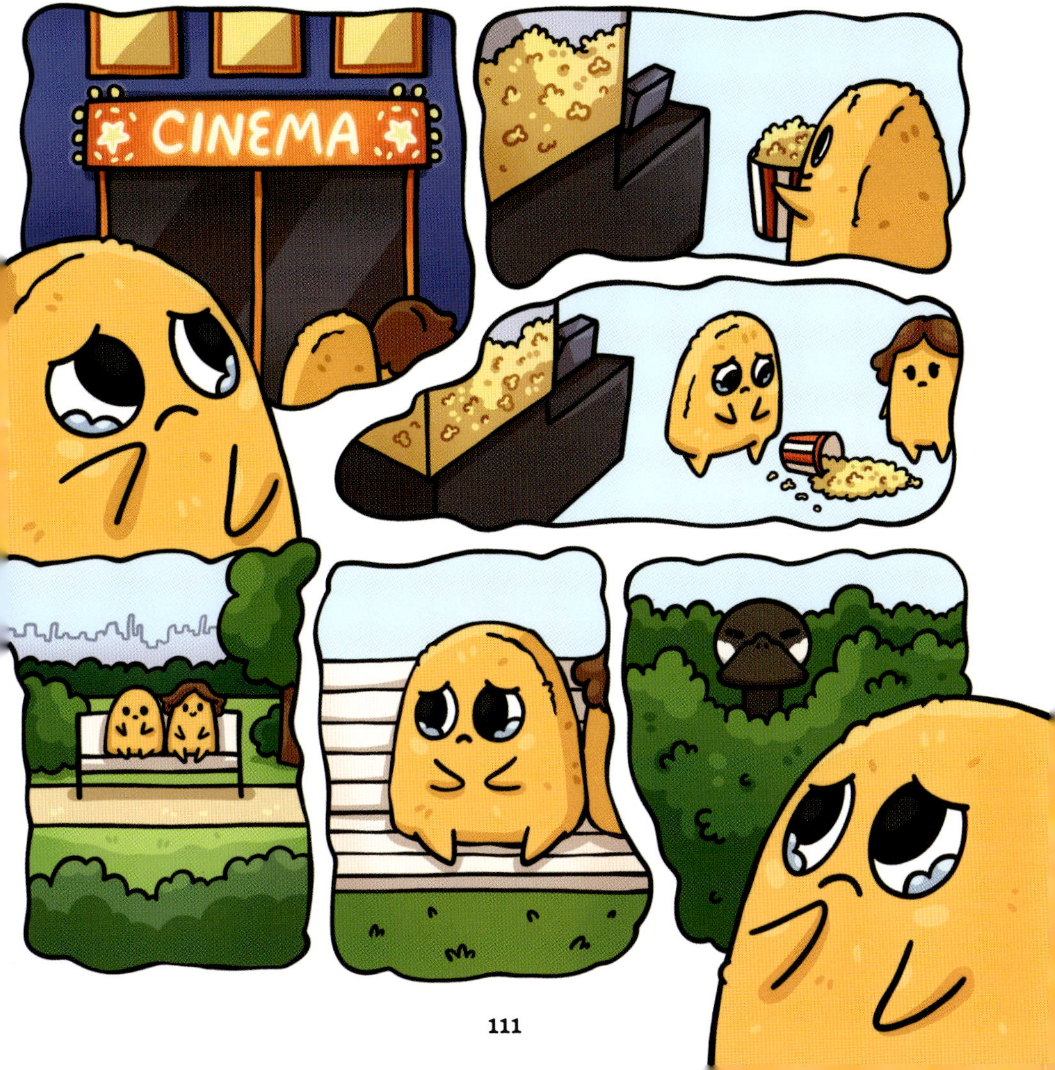
CINEMA

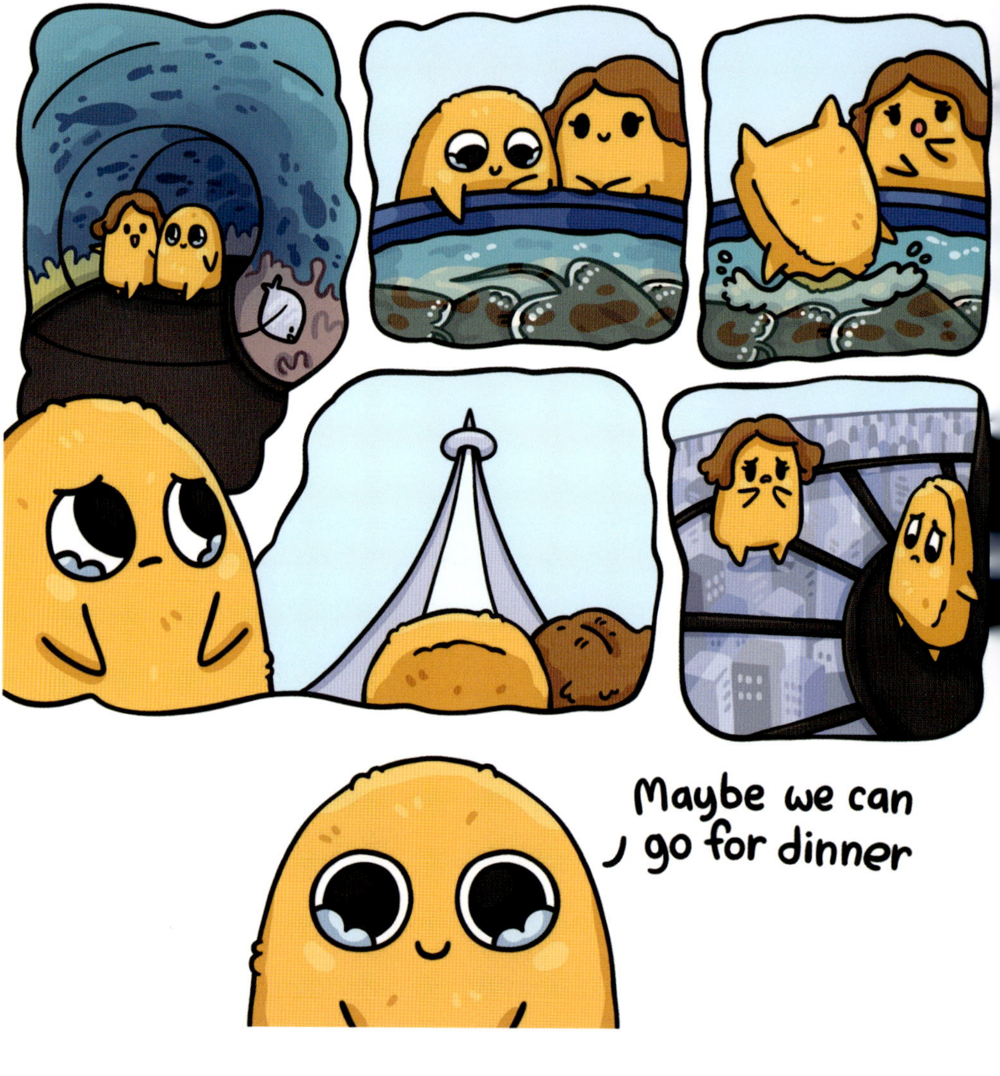
Maybe we can go for dinner

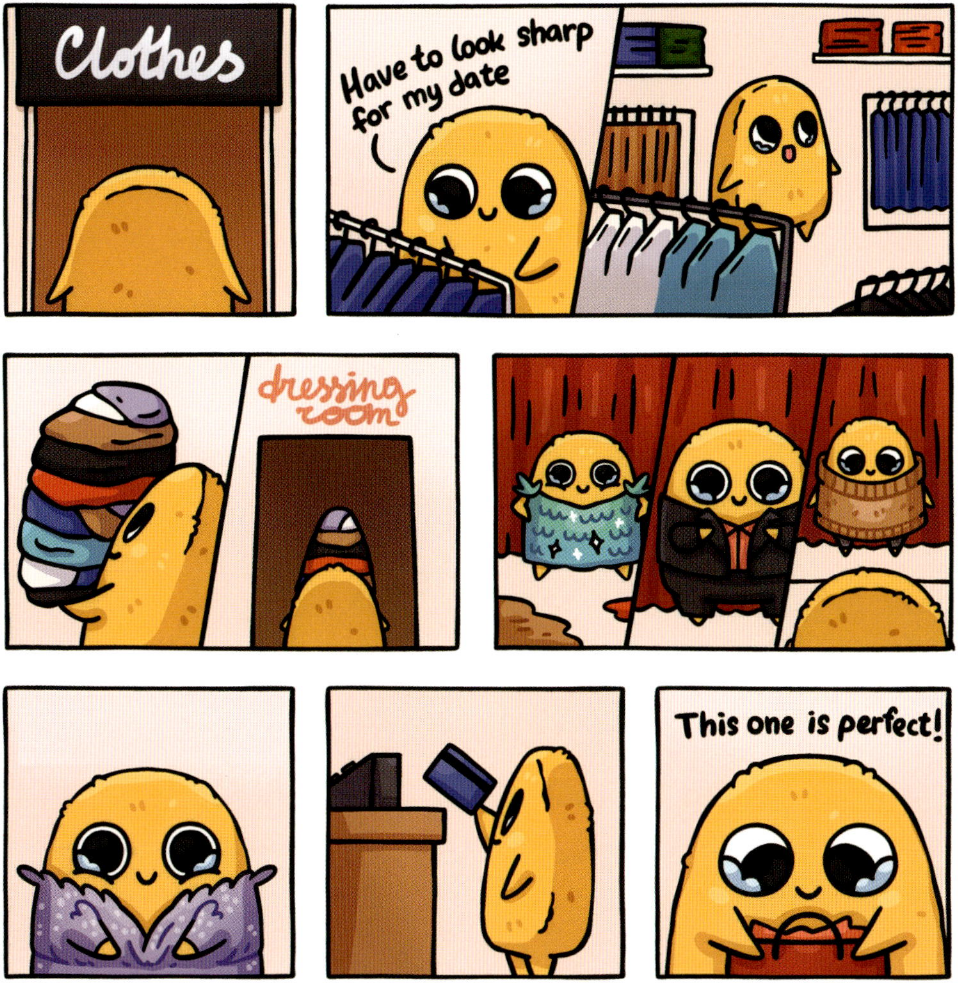
Clothes
Have to look sharp for my date
dressing room
This one is perfect!

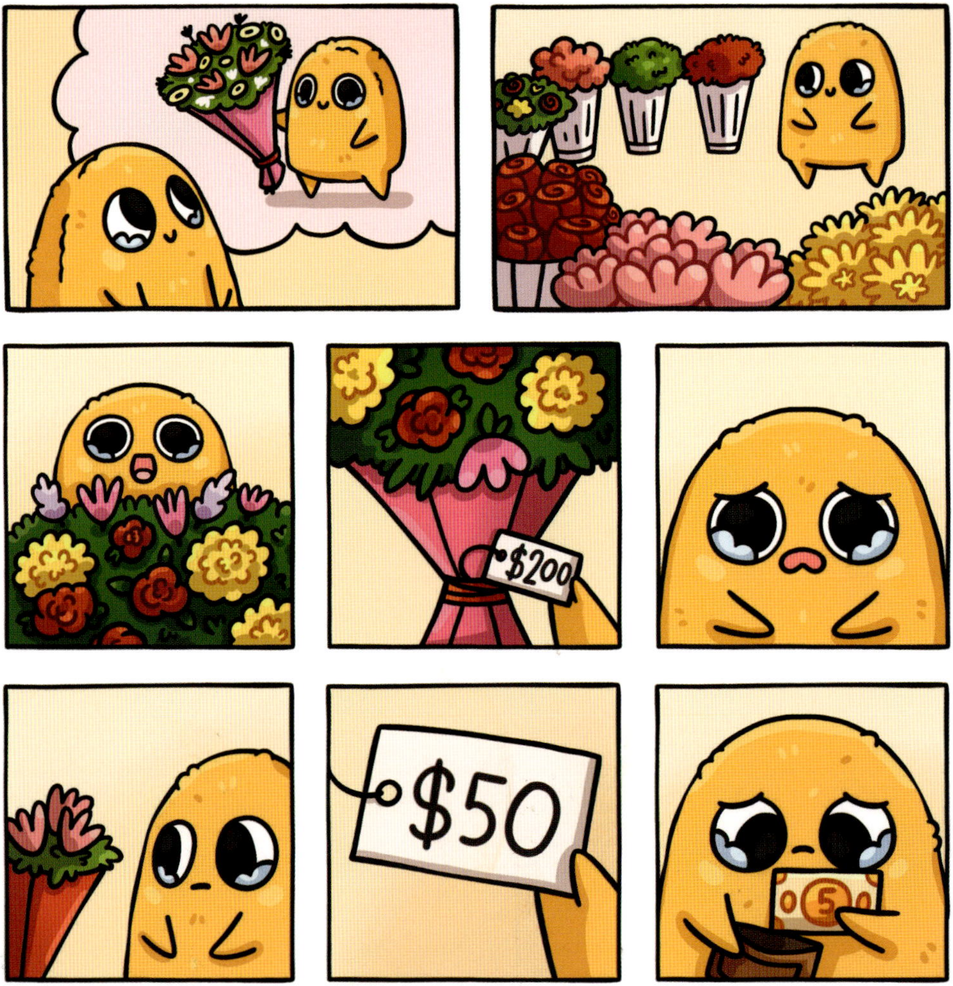
$200
$50

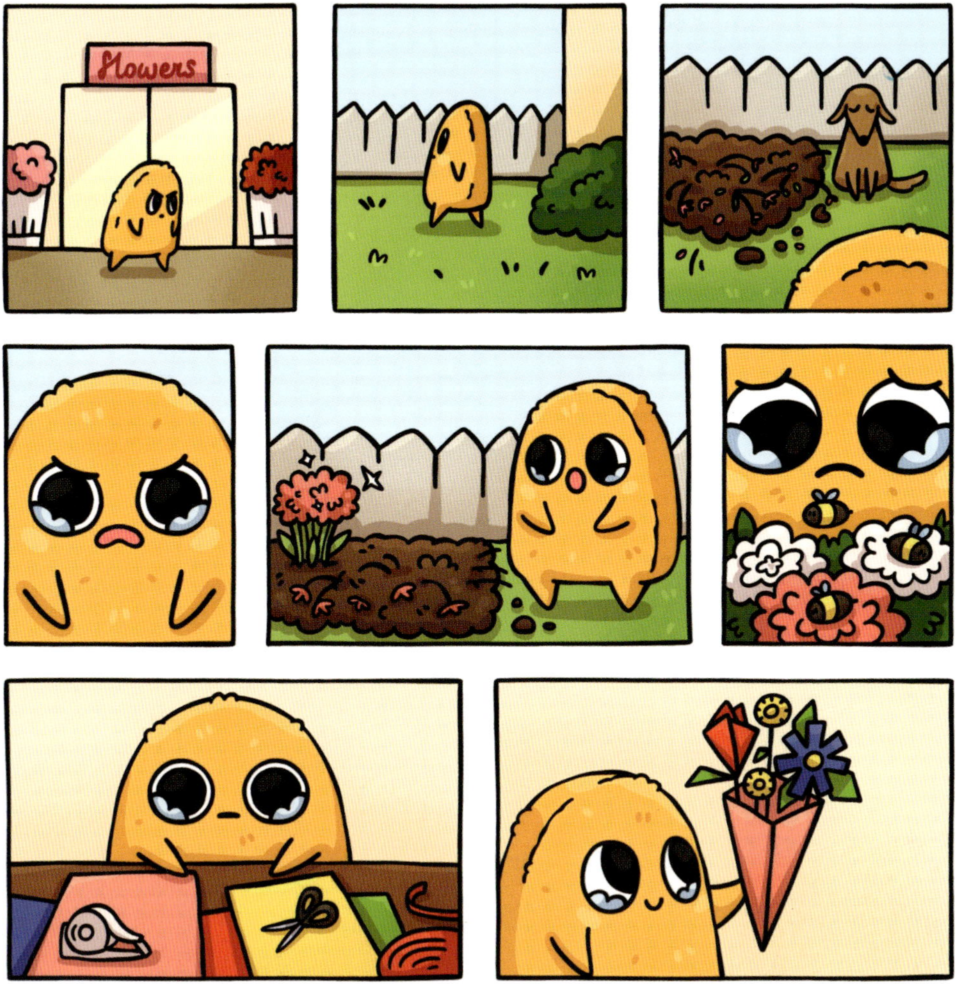
Flowers

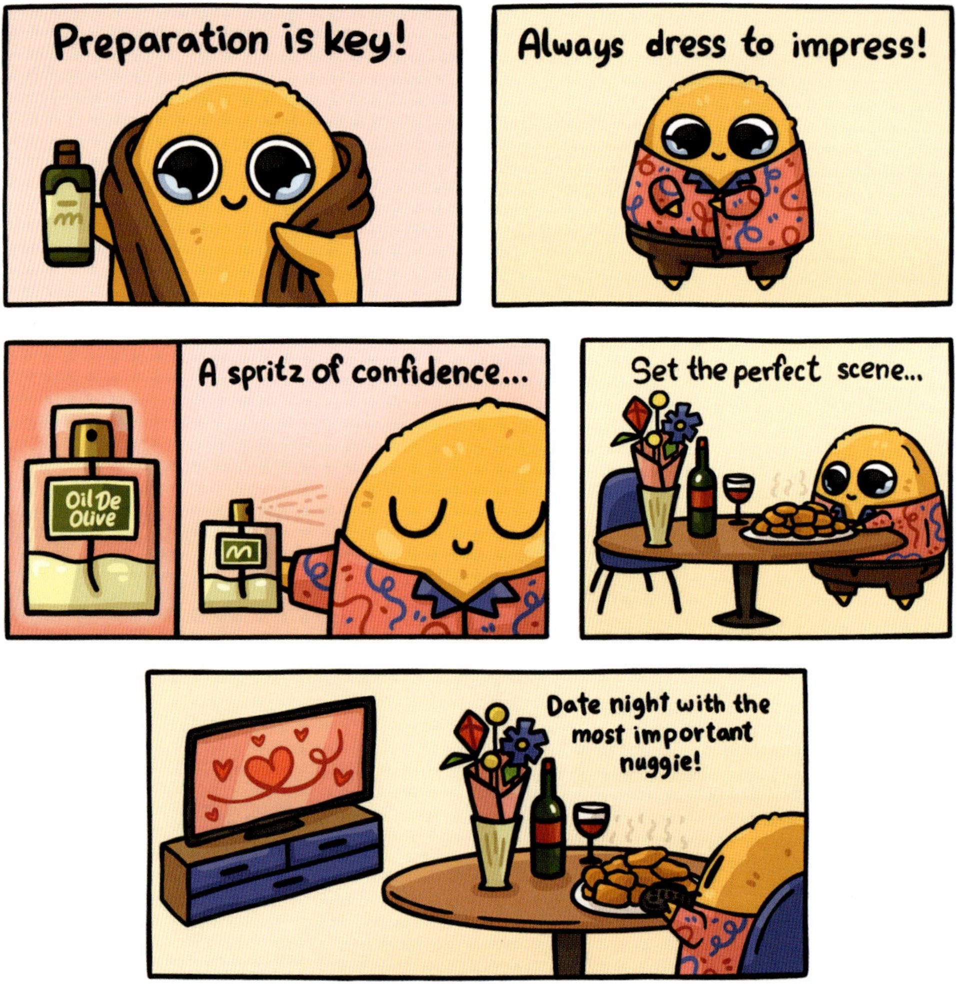
Preparation is key!
m
Always dress to impress!
Oil De Olive
A spritz of confidence...
m
Set the perfect scene...
Date night with the most important nuggie!

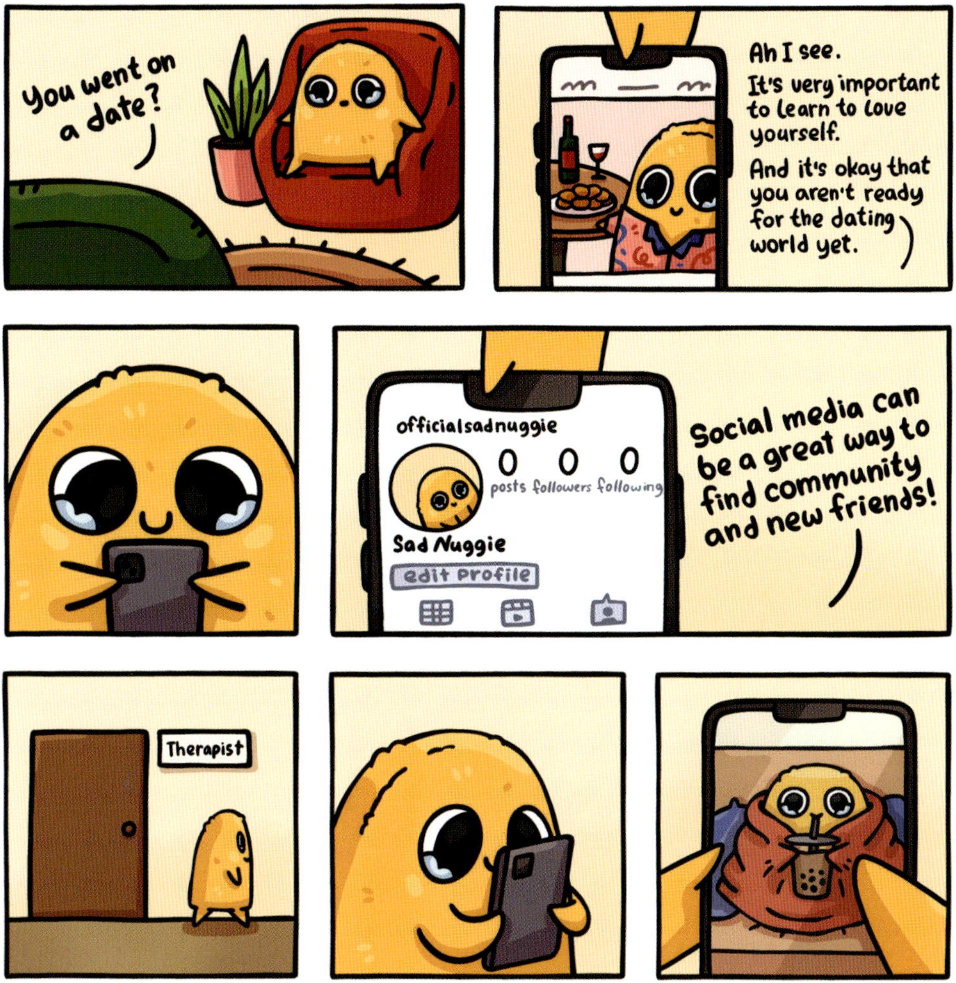
You went on a date?
Ah I see.
It's very important to learn to love yourself.
And it's okay that you aren't ready for the dating world yet.
officialsadnuggie
0 posts 0 followers 0 following
Sad Nuggie
edit profile
Social media can be a great way to find community and new friends!
Therapist

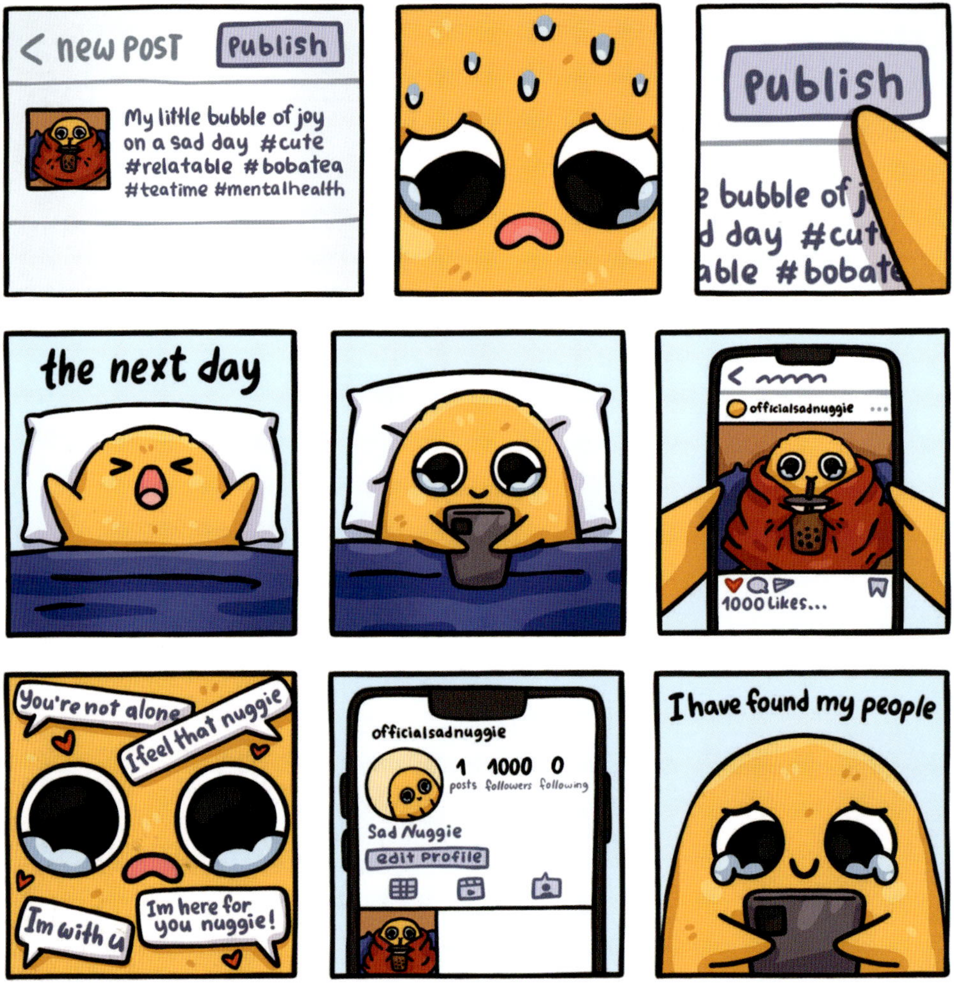
< new POST
Publish
My little bubble of joy on a sad day #cute #relatable #bobatea #teatime #mentalhealth
Publish
the next day
officialsadnuggie
1000 Likes...
You're not alone
I feel that nuggie
Im with u
Im here for you nuggie!
officialsadnuggie
1 posts
1000 followers
0 following
Sad Nuggie
edit profile
I have found my people

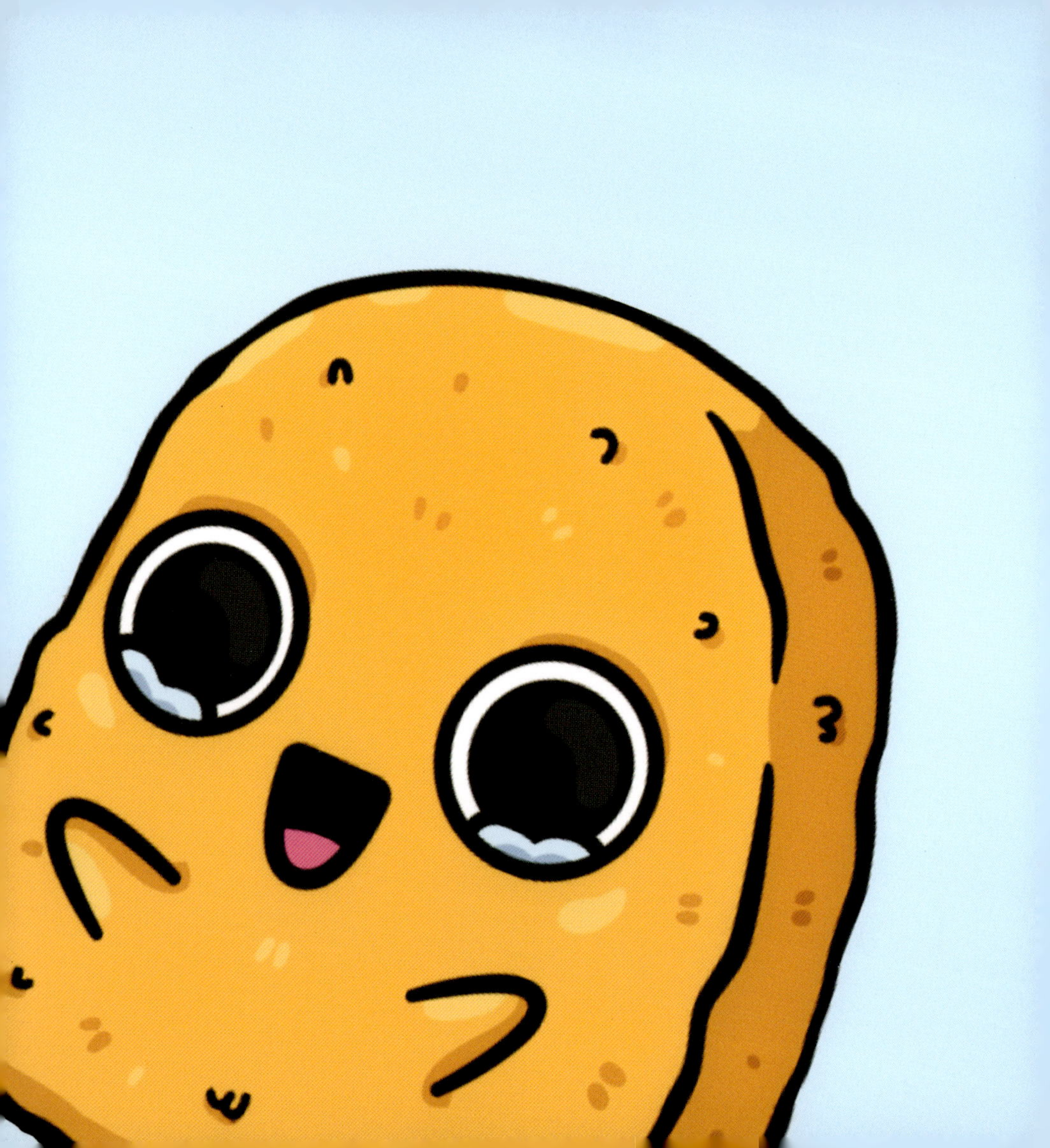

Meet Sad Nuggie

The world's favorite sad chicken nugget who brings smiles and laughter to people all around the world. Sad Nuggie is known for his lovable, relatable, and adorable personality. He may be constantly stressed and depressed, but he wishes nothing but the best for all his friends. If you ever need someone to talk to, Sad Nuggie is always there.

About the Brand

Sad Nuggie™ was officially launched on August 1, 2022. Sad Nuggie is dedicated to bringing smiles to everyone around the world with a wide variety of cute products, relatable and humorous comics, adorable memes, and more!

Since launch, Sad Nuggie gifs, videos, and images have been seen and shared more than one billion times around the world.

@officialsadnuggie

About the Illustrator

Anastasia Sevastyanova, known as @sevastasi, has been a dedicated freelance digital illustrator since 2019. With a rich portfolio, she has lent her artistic prowess to numerous children's and young adult books. Her expertise extends into character design and sticker art, with the iconic Sad Nuggie standing out as a testament to her passion and dedication. Anastasia approaches her craft with meticulous care, infusing each project with a profound love for her work. Her journey in the realm of digital illustration reflects a commitment to excellence and a genuine passion for bringing stories to life visually.

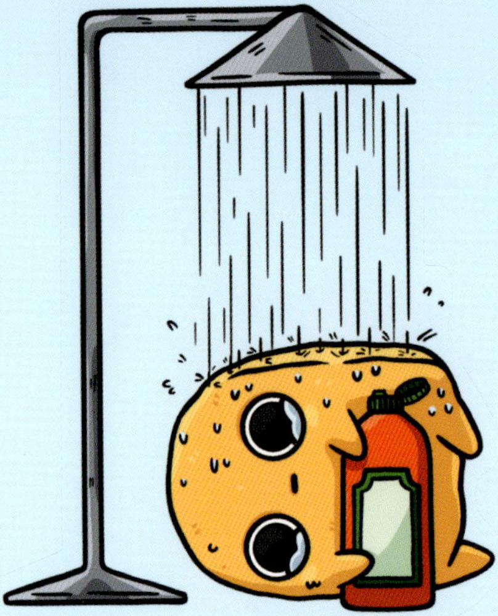
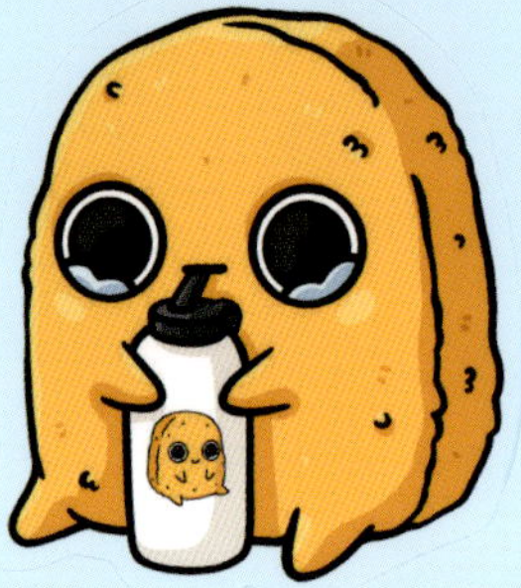
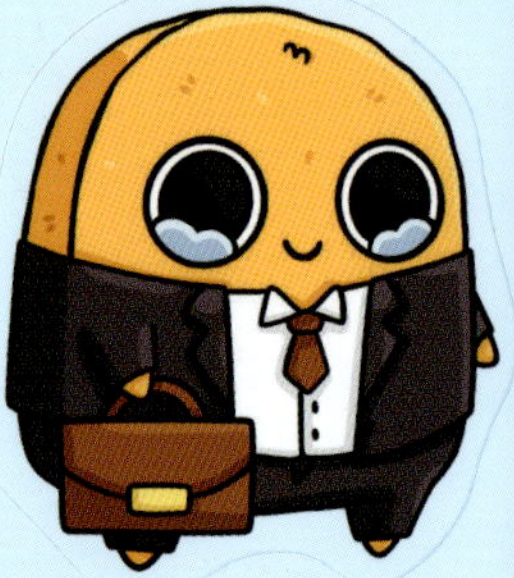
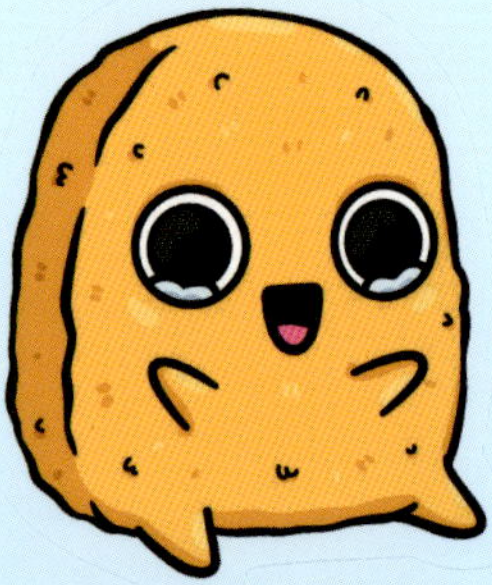
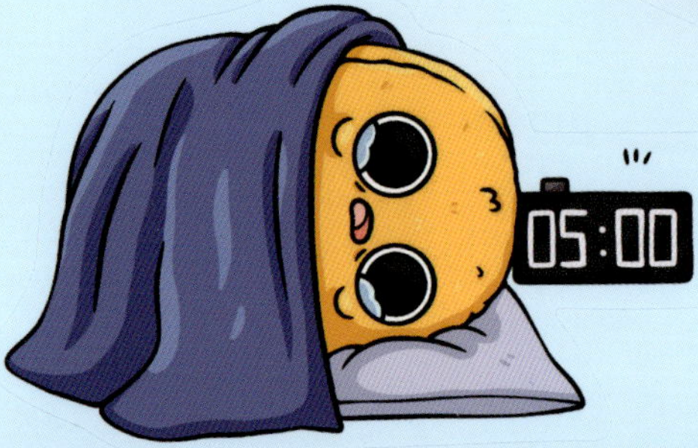
05:00
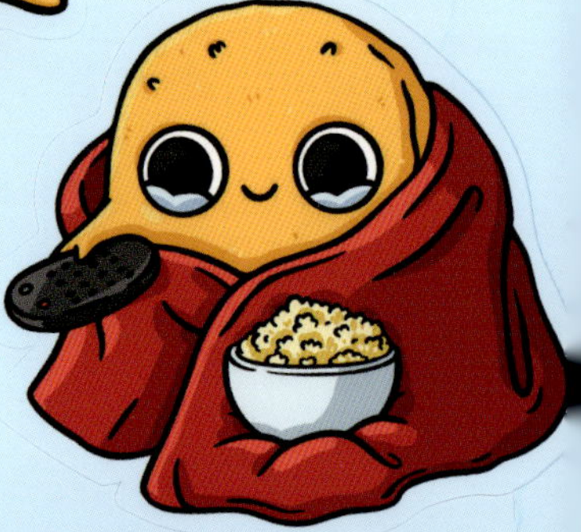

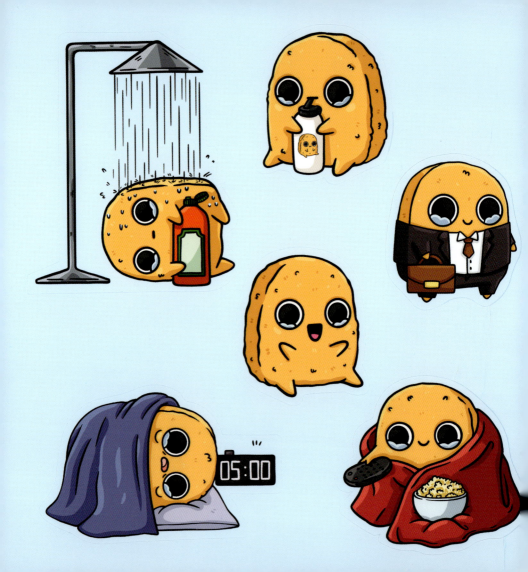

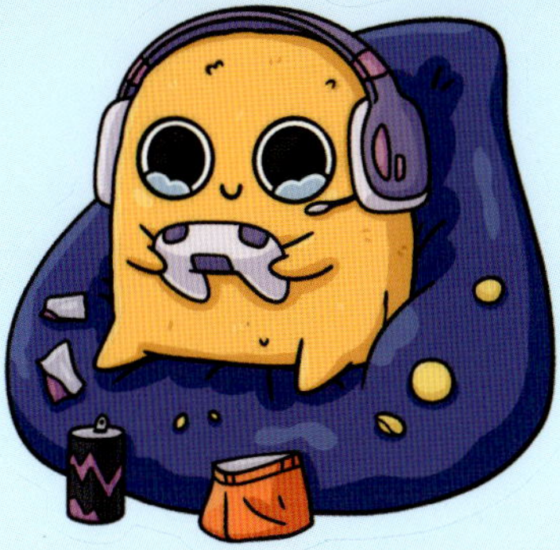
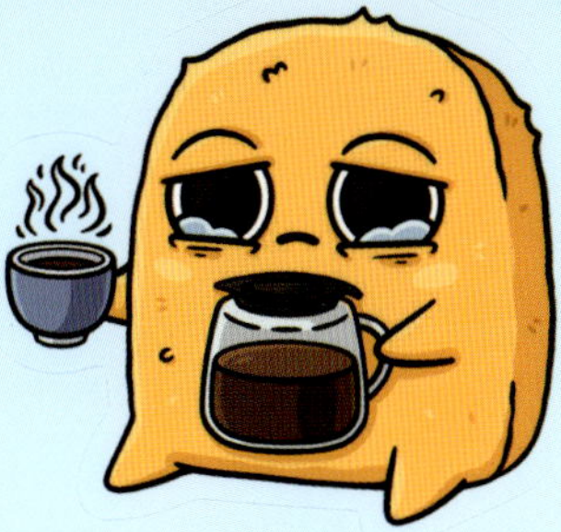
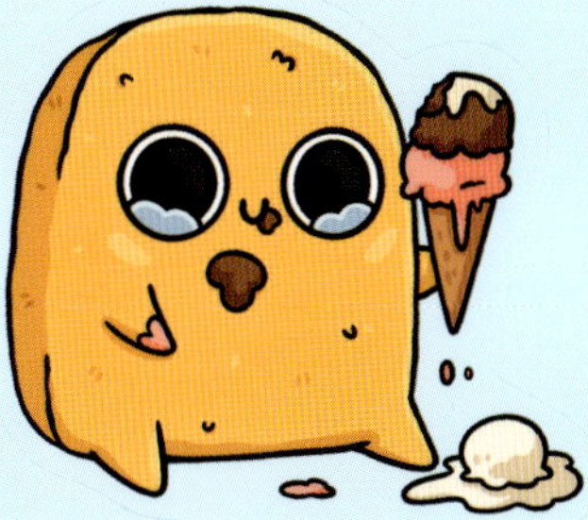
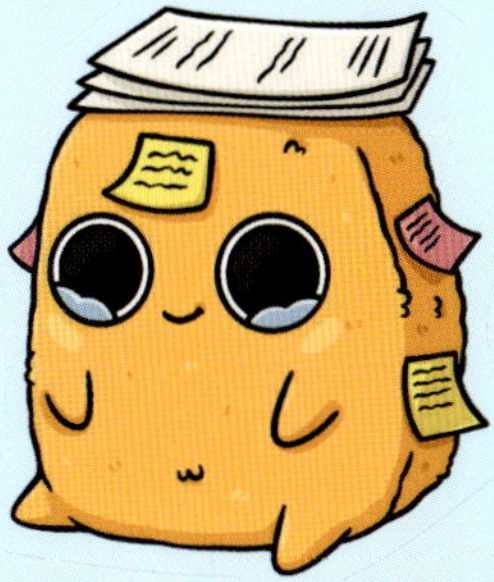
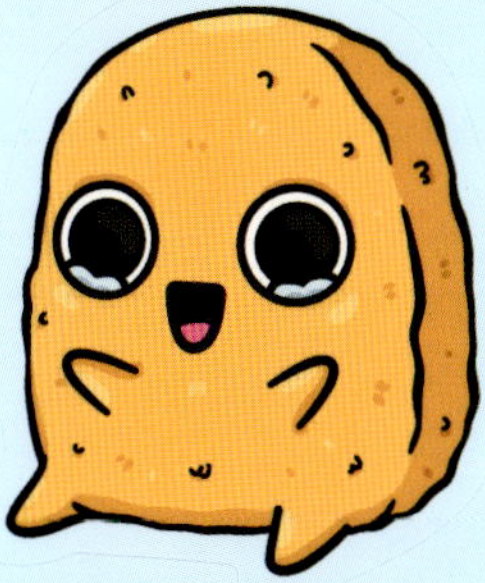
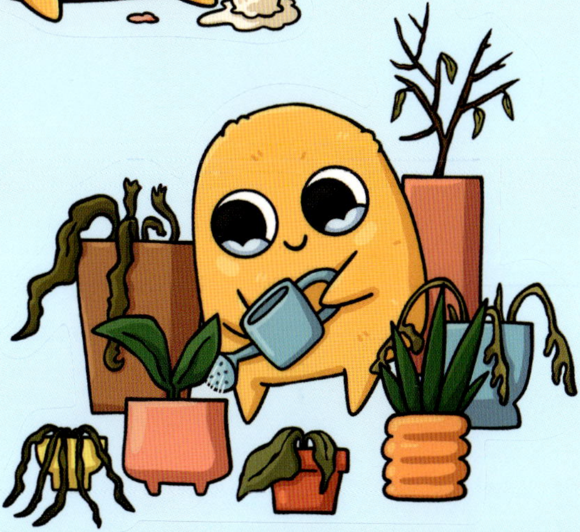

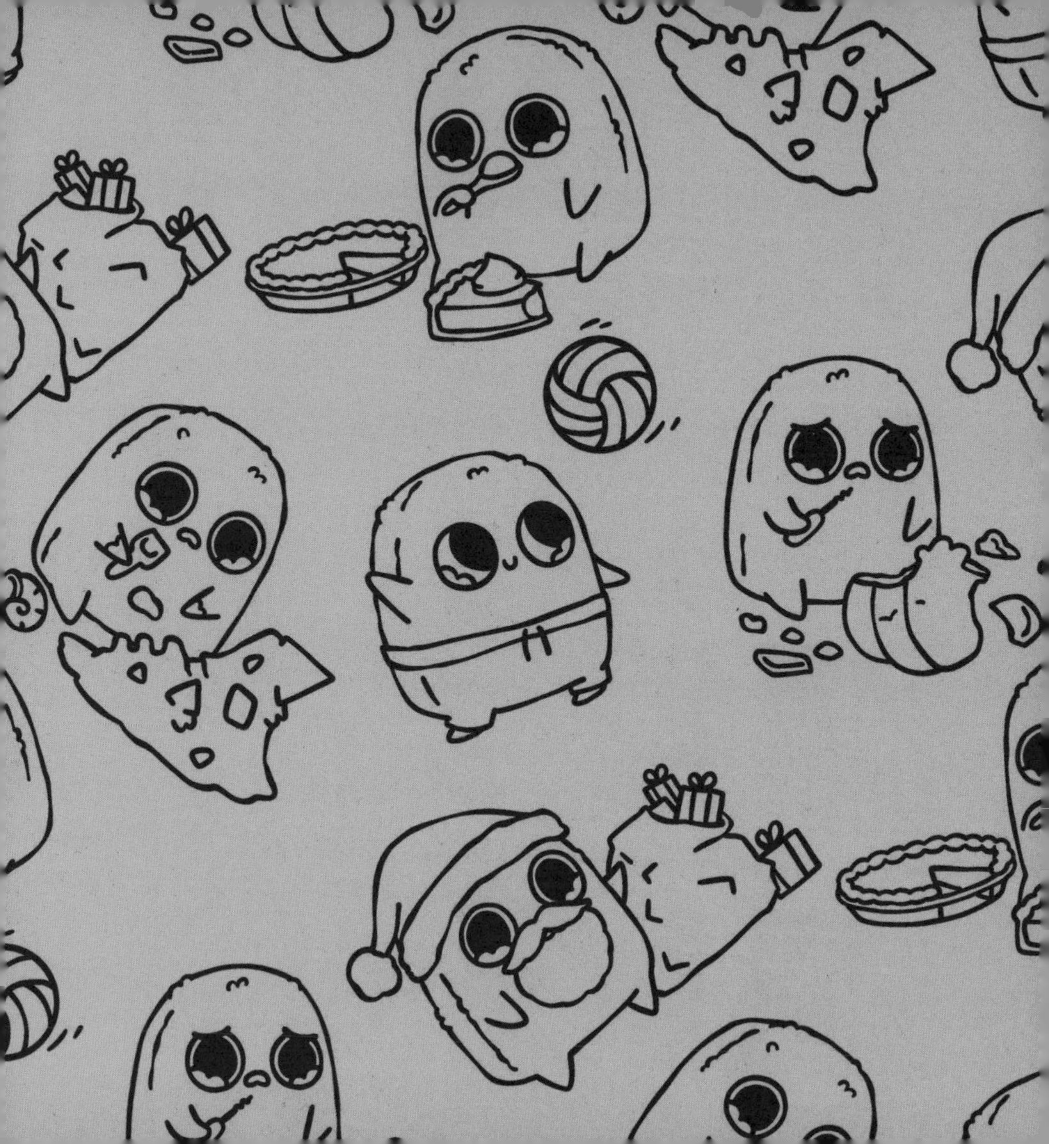

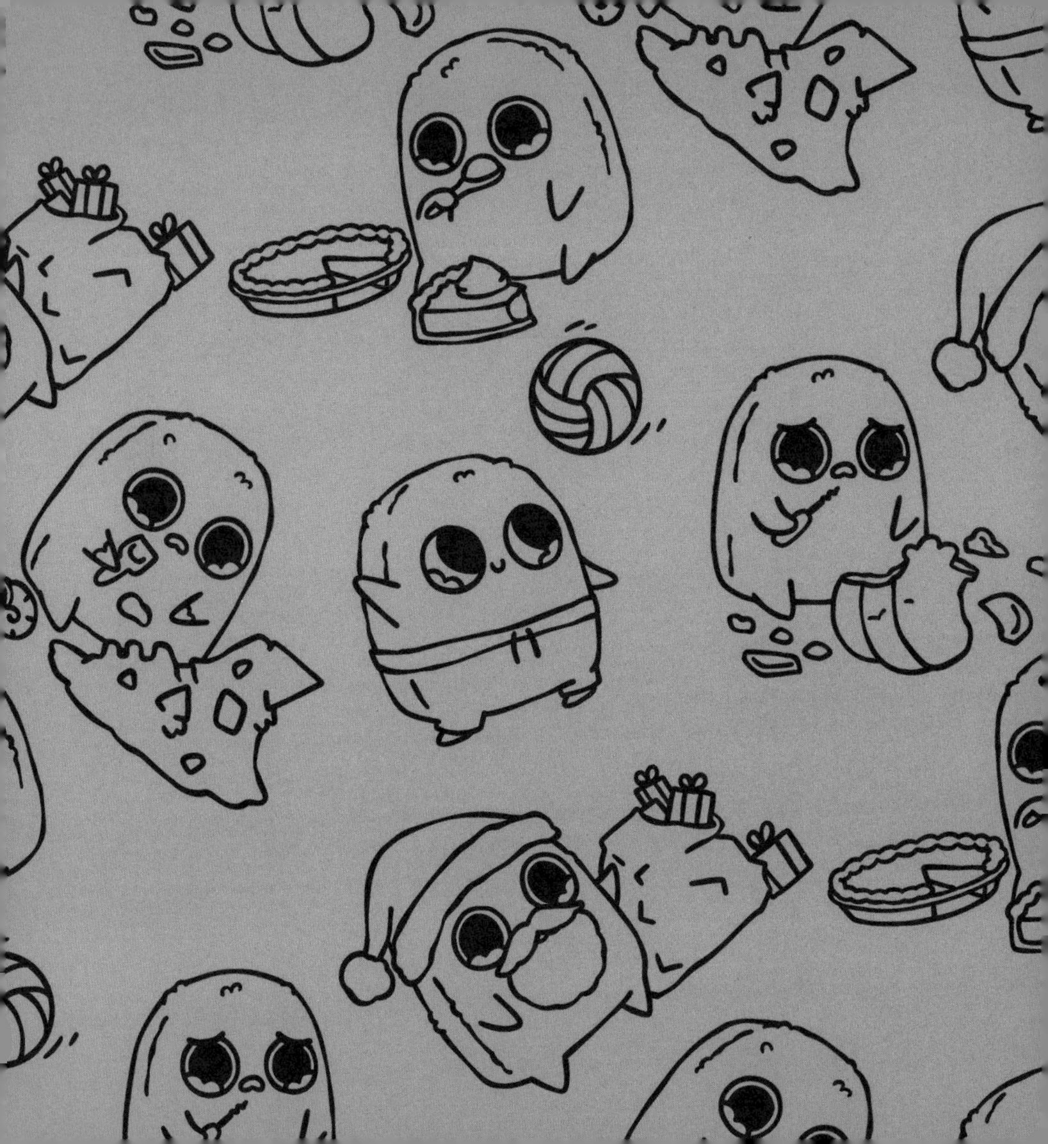